WITHDRAWN FROM

KING ALFR

GOD

& THE BIOLOGIST

|7

}

KA 0239643 2

GOD
&
THE BIOLOGIST

FAITH AT THE FRONTIERS
OF SCIENCE

R. J. BERRY

APOLLOS (an imprint of Inter-Varsity Press),
38 De Montfort Street, Leicester LE1 7GP, England

© R. J. Berry, 1996

All rights reserved. No part of this publication may be reproduced, stored in a
retrieval system, or transmitted, in any form or by any means, electronic,
mechanical, photocopying, recording or otherwise, without the prior
permission of the publisher or the Copyright Licensing Agency.

Unless otherwise stated, Scripture quotations in this publication are from the
Holy Bible, New International Version. Copyright © 1973, 1978, 1984 by
International Bible Society. Used by permission of Hodder & Stoughton Ltd.
All rights reserved. 'NIV' is a registered trademark of International Bible
Society. UK trademark number 1448790.

First published 1996

British Library Cataloguing in Publication Data
A catalogue record for this book is available from the British Library.

ISBN 0–85111–446–6

Set in Garamond No. 3

Typeset in Great Britain by Parker Typesetting Service, Leicester

Printed in Great Britain by Clays Ltd, Bungay, Suffolk

KING ALFRED'S COLLEGE
WINCHESTER

01774615
02-396732

CONTENTS

PREFACE   vii

1 *Context*   1
2 *Reason*   11
3 *Evolution and purpose*   29
4 *Genes and Genesis*   59
5 *Environmental ethics*   85
6 *Affirmation*   109

FURTHER READING   127

BIBLIOGRAPHY   129

INDEX   139

PREFACE

The contents of this book formed the 1994 Pascal Lectures on Christianity and the University, at the University of Waterloo, Ontario. They were delivered also at the University of British Columbia at the invitation of the Graduate and Faculty Christian Forum at that university. Although I have expanded the text from the spoken version, what follows should not be regarded as a definitive work of scholarship. My intention was – and is – to clear away the overgrown thickets which confuse and deter those who want to explore the interface of science and faith, where (importantly) the world of the spirit meets the world of the flesh and experience. I refer where relevant to authorities and reviews relating to the matters I deal with, but the pedant wanting every 'i' dotted and every 't' crossed will have to search elsewhere than this account.

My aims are specific and limited: to show that there need be no barriers between real science and real faith; to remove some of the stumbling-blocks which lead many to assume that science has somehow disproved or discredited religion, or that faith is difficult or impossible in a scientific age; and to revisit some of the murky areas surrounding assumptions about creation and life, particularly those about where God fits into scientific understanding.

My title, *God and the Biologist*, is chosen for three reasons. First, the lectures were a personal account of how I, as a Christian biologist, have dealt with the problems of science and belief in my own life. By profession, I am an ecological geneticist, so I have had to face whether evolution and creation are contradictory or complementary, and (I believe more urgently) what should be the Christian doctrine of creation in the finite and degraded world in which we live. Because I deal with living organisms, I have had to ask myself what 'life' is, and this leads to questions about genetic manipulation and the proper approach to the so-called 'new reproductive technologies' (*in vitro* fertilization, artificial insemination, and so on). Is there a theology of DNA?

I have not attempted to cover all the questions at the interface of biological science and religious belief. I say little (for example) about the nature of consciousness or behavioural modification of brain function. These are topics which I have never had to face at first hand, and I have refrained from a theoretical consideration of them. I justify this on the grounds that this is a personal account of one biologist's journey. Notwithstanding, I have tried to deal with the principles of how Christians should develop their attitude to new discoveries and technologies so that a reader of the three case-studies in this book (evolution, genetic manipulation and environmental ethics, which form chapters 3, 4 and 5 respectively) can work towards a true Christian maturity (Rom. 12:2) (Stott 1992).

Secondly, people sometimes express surprise that a scientist can be a Christian. Having recovered from that (there is probably as high a proportion of scientists who are Christians as, say, hairdressers or bank clerks), they then recall that they have heard speak or read the writings of a Christian physicist or a Christian engineer. I do not believe that faith is more difficult for biologists than for physicists, but merely that physicists have been more assiduous in describing their faith than biologists. One of the most erudite contemporary apologists for Christianity is John Polkinghorne, formerly Professor of Mathematical Physics at Cambridge University. He has recently summarized much of his earlier writing in a book entitled *The Faith of a Physicist* (1994) (that is the US title; in the UK it is called *Science and Christian Belief*). In similar vein, this book is about the faith of a biologist.

Thirdly, the contentious subjects in the area of science and faith used to be those concerned with the world as a machine – determinism, miracles and so on. This focus has now shifted to biological questions – such as the nature of the mind, the ethics of sex, the natural world and the meaning of wilderness. But the underlying question is still 'Where does God fit into scientific knowledge and understanding?' – if indeed he does fit. The difference is that the debates are now more about ethics and responsibility than the rather more recondite arguments of the nineteenth and early twentieth centuries. This makes it particularly important for Christian biologists to contribute in the arena of science and faith. Chapter 1 of this book sets the scene for this contribution, leading on to a consideration of some general principles of interpretation (chapter 2) which is a necessary preliminary to the specifically biological topics of chapters 3, 4 and 5.

In preparing my lectures, I inevitably drew on work I have previously published, especially *Real Science, Real Faith* (1991) in chapter 1; *Adam and the Ape* (1975, revised as *God and Evolution*, 1988) in chapters 2 and 3; 'The Theology of DNA' (*Anvil* 4:39–49, 1987) in chapter 4; and 'Green Religion and Green Science' (*Journal of the Royal Society of Arts* 141:305–318, 1993a) and 'Creation and the Environment' (*Science and Christian Belief* 7:21–43, 1995) in chapter 5. I am grateful for permission to quote from these sources.

My thanks are due also to Brigadier Ian Dobbie, Sir Timothy Hoare, the Most Reverend Richard Holloway, the Reverend Bob Mardsen, and Sir Ghillean Prance FRS for reading parts of this book; their comments have helped to make some points much clearer than they would otherwise have been, although I remain, of course, responsible for all the infelicities and interpretations. Finally, I am indebted to those who invited me to lecture and looked after me in Canada, forcing me to prepare this book for publication, particularly Professors Philip Hill and Edward Piers and Dr Bart van der Kamp in Vancouver, and Mrs Joan Hadley and Professor Graham Gladwell in Waterloo. Permission to reproduce passages from Donald MacKay's booklet *Science and Christian Faith Today* has been given by Dr Valerie MacKay; to reprint Norman Nicholson's poem on Genesis 1:1 by Elizabeth Duggan of David Higham Associates; and Robert Rendall's 'Orkney Crofter' by Mr R. P. Rendall of Aberdeen.

R. J. Berry

1

CONTEXT

Science without religion is lame, religion without science is blind.

Albert Einstein

Some years ago, I was one of the signatories of a letter about miracles to *The Times* of London (13 July 1984). The reason for the letter was the reported comments of a prominent churchman that no educated person could believe in miracles; any such belief was a hangover from a prescientific age when we knew far less about the cause of natural events than we do now. Fourteen of us signed the letter: we were all professors of science in British universities, and six were fellows of the Royal Society. We were explicit about the weakness of the case against miracles:

> It is not logically valid to use science as an argument against miracles. To believe that miracles cannot happen is as much an act of faith as to believe that they can happen. We gladly accept the virgin birth, the Gospel miracles and the resurrection of Christ as historical . . . Miracles are unprecedented events. Whatever the current fashions in philosophy or the revelations of the opinion polls may suggest, it is important to affirm that science (based as it is upon the observation of precedents) can have nothing to say on the subject. Its 'laws' are only generalisations of our experience . . .

A week later, an article appeared in the science journal *Nature* (310:171, 19 July 1994), accepting our statement about the nature of scientific laws, but dissenting from our conclusion about miracles. It called them 'inexplicable and irreproducible phenomena [which] do not occur – a definition by exclusion of the concept . . . the publication of Berry *et al.* provides a licence not merely for religious belief (which on other grounds is unexceptional) but for mischievous reports of all things paranormal, from ghosts to flying saucers.'

This criticism prompted a number of replies, mostly agreeing with us, and dissenting from the Editor's assumptions. For example, P. G. H. Clarke, writing from Switzerland, objected:

> Your concern not to license 'mischievous reports of all things paranormal' is no doubt motivated in the interest of scientific truth, but your strategy of defining away what you find unpalatable is the antithesis of scientific. It is disheartening that *Nature* should sell its empiricist birthright for the stale soup of *a priori* rationalism.

Donald MacKay, a distinguished Scottish brain scientist, wrote,

> If, as Christians have traditionally believed, the whole spatio-temporal sequence of events that make up our world owes its being to our Creator, then it is thanks to Him that our scientific explanations normally prove as reliable as they do. But by the same token nothing whatever in our observation of 'normal precedents' can make it impossible for the Creator to bring about a totally unprecedented event, if His overall purpose for His creation requires it.

He went on to make an important assertion:

> For the Christian believer, baseless credulity is a sin – a disservice to the God of truth. His belief in the resurrection does not stem from softness in his standards of evidence, but rather from the coherence with which (as he sees it) that particular unprecedented event fits into and makes sense of a great mass of data . . . Both wishful thinking and wishful unthinking are evils.

Having published a clutch of such letters, the Editor than asked me to write a 3,000-word article on miracles, which he published (*Nature* 322:321–322, 25 July 1986) under the heading 'What to Believe about Miracles'. (My proposed title was less presumptuous; it was 'Miracles: Scepticism, Credulity or Reality?') This produced its own crop of responses, including an examination of the subject by William Kruskal in his Presidential Address to the American Statistical Association

(Kruskal 1988) and a letter to me from a leading US biologist saying that the only miracle to him was 'that *Nature* would publish such dreary bullshit'.

It is not my purpose to pursue this (or any other) debate about miracles in any depth but to use it to make two points. First, although grandiose claims are sometimes made that 'science has disproved religion' (or something along those lines), the fact is that science meets faith at only three points: origins, miracles, and the nature of human beings – and all three of them are concerned with the relationship of God (if there is one) with the natural world. Any significant enquiry into the reasonableness of faith in the modern world has to begin and end with this relationship; the difficulty about making such an enquiry is that both science and faith have their own independent stories about origins, miracles and humans, and take a lot of persuading that their account is not complete and sufficient.

Secondly, science is concerned with reality. Philosophers (and for that matter, physicists) argue for hours about what may be reality and objectivity. We are told we can never *know* something absolutely and that any event is modified by our observation of it. Notwithstanding, we should not allow ourselves to be distracted by clever arguments; there actually is a real world 'out there'. We may misapprehend it and misinterpret it, but it is indubitably there with its own properties and limitations. We are not free to ignore this world or to treat its existence as a purely academic exercise (Helm 1987). For many centuries there was a firm assumption that the whole world from the motion of falling bodies to the existence of God could be understood by pure thought: philosophers and theologians strove to derive proofs of the existence of God; thinkers such as Plato declared that nature worked according to certain principles, and sought to deduce from these principles the phenomena of the whole natural world. Scholasticism changed into science when facts became important, and the notion that theories could be developed independently of the facts was abandoned. It was a revolution conventionally dated to beginning in 1543, when the very different works of Copernicus on astronomy and Vesalius on anatomy were published, and the attitudes in them began to take hold.

Put crudely, we need to understand and examine the world in which we live, and to ask ourselves whether scientists can tell us all there is to know about it or whether there are questions which science cannot answer. If there are such questions, where do we turn for answers?

This is the intellectual context in which we live. What about the personal context? Here, of course, we cannot easily generalize, because personal experiences are by definition subjective. Let me digress to describe my own history, not because I regard it as having importance to anyone but myself, but because it shows how apparently unrelated and unpleasant events can be seen in retrospect to fall into a clear pattern. The key for me was the suicide of my father when I was seventeen. I had been sent to boarding-school because my mother was incapacitated with multiple sclerosis; as I was an only child my father thought it better for me to be away from home. Because of my mother's illness, my father and I were particularly close, and his suicide was proportionately more difficult for me to understand. My memory is of coming home for the inquest and funeral, and going for long walks by myself, asking, 'Why? Why? Why?' I don't know if I was a real Christian at that time. When I joined the Boy Scouts, I had been told that I ought to go to church because my Scout's promise included a commitment to 'honour God'. I used to haul my father along on most Sundays to a dreary and incomprehensible ritual at our local parish church. I took my confirmation (at boarding-school) seriously, and later learned that on the Sunday before the confirmation service the school chaplain had preached on the text, 'Here I am! I [Jesus] stand at the door and knock. If anyone hears my voice and opens the door, I will come in' (Rev. 3:20). I remember the occasion, and know that I followed the steps in the exposition. But three years later, I could discern no meaning in life or understand why my father decided to take his life 'while the balance of his mind was temporarily disturbed through overwork'.

The summer after my father's death I went to a houseparty run by a Christian organization. There I heard that the death of Jesus Christ at Calvary was not simply the end of an inspired teacher or the defeat of a promising liberation movement, but was God's intervention to provide a way back into his purpose for all who accepted him at his word – and there was no reason why that should not include me. In a hackneyed phrase, everything fell into place. The explanation of the New Testament events was intellectually satisfying and blindingly obvious. Like Thomas Henry Huxley a century earlier, who commented on reading Darwin's *Origin of Species*, 'How stupid not to have thought of that oneself', I was rationally convinced of what, I later discovered, was the Christian gospel of salvation through grace alone.

My acceptance of Christ as my Saviour is relevant because it was to me on that August day in 1952 a completely logical response to a reasoned argument on a par with the rigour expected in my high-school science studies (indeed, looking back it has remained so ever since). I had planned to be a doctor and already had a provisional offer of a place in the medical school at Cambridge University. A few months later, I realized that I would not be happy spending my life coping with other people at first hand, and, in the first event which, in retrospect, showed me God's nudging Spirit, I changed from a medical to a biology course.

As a Christian at university, I was faced with a hierarchy of possibilities. The really holy people became missionaries, the rather holy people were ordained, and the fairly holy ones became teachers; the also-rans did all the other jobs in the world. I hope I was prepared to serve abroad if God wanted me there, but I felt no particular call. I was tempted to train for the Church of England ministry, but two weeks of 'testing my vocation' proved to me that God did not want me in that job; just as I would have been a terrible doctor, I would also have been a disastrous parson. So I started applying for school teaching posts – but no-one offered me a job. I assumed God had a purpose for my life, but it wasn't very clear. The line of least resistance was to do the minimum. I stayed in the university world, working for a PhD in genetics at University College London. And, despite having pushed a few doors, I have remained in the university world; since 1974 I have been Professor of Genetics in the University of London.

Linked to the false assumption about the sanctity of various jobs that was around in my Cambridge days was a parallel belief that all Christians were supposed to be evangelists. My problem was that I had none of the gifts possessed by some of getting alongside people and proclaiming Christ. It was a great relief when I realized that we have all been given different talents and callings, and that there is not (and should not be) such a thing as a typical or normal Christian. This is not an excuse to avoid living and speaking for Christ at every appropriate opportunity; rather it is a recognition that (in the words of the Westminster Confession) 'the chief end of man is to glorify God and to enjoy him for ever', which does not necessarily mean that we are supposed primarily to operate as more or less full-time evangelists.

Looking back, it took me some time to accept that I was in a place that God had prepared for me. After all, making microscopical preparations of mouse embryos (which was the main practical work in my PhD studies), or catching radioactive rats in India, or melanic moths in Shetland, or limpets in the Antarctic, is not usually considered to be a spiritual activity. But I have no doubt that God has wanted me as a scientist, and that he has given me work to do for him because I was in the place he had prepared for me.

Evolutionary biology

When I first began to learn biology at school, it appeared to be a hotchpotch of facts and ideas – interesting but disconnected. Only when we were introduced to evolution did everything start to make sense; it became possible to recognize patterns in classification, distribution, development and biological history. It was the same at university. By then I was vaguely aware of the nineteenth-century debates about Genesis and evolution, but they remained shadowy until a medical-student friend whom I had taken to hear a number of evangelistic sermons informed me that it would be intellectually dishonest for him to become a Christian because he 'would not be allowed to believe in evolution'. Of course I told him that was nonsense, that neither belief nor disbelief in evolution had anything to do with his relationship with the crucified Christ, but he would not be swayed.

I suspect that my friend's views about evolution were an excuse to avoid commitment – although they were real to him at the time. But they made me go back both to the Bible creation stories and to the history of the controversy about creation and evolution. It rapidly became clear to me that much of the argument has been about interpretation rather than basic doctrine, and that much of the heat in the creation debate comes from improper extrapolation from the Bible text itself or is about secondary issues (what may be called 'evolutionism', owing more to Herbert Spencer's speculative social Darwinism than to the biological ideas of Charles Darwin himself). As a scientist, I have no doubt whatsoever that evolutionary change has occurred and that its mechanism is along the lines described by neo-Darwinian theory; as a Christian, I am equally confident that God created the world and everything in it, and that all holds together in him. The Genesis account of creation is of a progress from nothing (or more strictly, God only) through geological and biological change to humankind. Nowhere in the Bible are we told the mechanisms God used to carry out his work; indeed it is only by faith that we know that God is involved (Heb. 11:3).

The main part of this book consists of three case-studies: on evolution, on human life issues, and on environmental ethics. We can learn a great deal from the debates on evolution (which are in many ways an exact rerun of the arguments that Galileo had with the church of the seventeenth century, and which the church of the nineteenth and twentieth centuries has conspicuously failed to learn). Chapter 2 is a general consideration of faith (especially Christianity) and science, chapter 3 is about evolution, chapter 4 about 'life' questions, and chapter 5 about the environment.

Professionally I am an ecological geneticist. Most of my research has been on the factors affecting and changing gene frequencies in natural populations (Berry 1977; Berry & Bradshaw 1992). This means that I am concerned with evolutionary mechanisms; I can be properly described as an evolutionary biologist. But the study of natural populations and their interactions is the science of ecology; I am as much an ecologist as a geneticist, and have indeed served in senior positions with several of the more important learned societies in ecology in Britain and Europe. And, as a Christian, I have properly been drawn into debates about the right and responsible use of the resources of this world from both the secular and the Christian point of view. I write in chapter 5 of my experience in national and international debates.

Finally, as a biologist I have inevitably been involved in discussions about the nature and treatment of life in general and human life in particular. For twenty years I was a member of the General Synod of the Church of England, and during that time chaired a working party to determine the Church of England's response to Government proposals to regulate new reproductive technologies – *in vitro* fertilization, embryo experimentation, and so on. Following extensive debate both within and outside Parliament, the British Parliament passed in 1990 an Act to regulate these activities; it is the first such comprehensive legislation in the world. The body appointed by the Government to implement this legislation is the Human Fertilization and Embryology Authority. I have been a member of this Authority since its beginning, and describe in chapter 4 some of its work and how a Christian can view it.

I have called this first chapter 'Context', and have sought to show that faith in God does not take place in a vacuum, but should be expressed in the world in which we live out our earthly span. I say 'should be expressed' because far too many people separate their spiritual life as much as possible from their everyday material life (Triton 1970). There is a long tradition of such an attitude, going at least as far back as the Stoics and Epicureans, who despised or feared the world, and justified their behaviour on their understanding of the nature of matter. Similar philosophies recur repeatedly down the centuries, formally justified by complicated philosophies and dignified by a host of names. There are many scientists who keep their religious and scientific lives in separate compartments, and never think through the implications of their faith. There are even more people who accept the assumptions of evangelistic agnostics like the Huxleys, J. B. S. Haldane or J. D. Bernal, and never explore the possibility that science has not disproved or overcome religion. And sadly there are religious people who speak against science in the belief that it is inevitably atheistic and therefore dangerous. The right way of dealing with such attitudes is to test the validity of the arguments used in such situations, and the bulk of this book is concerned with three case-studies of apparent conflict between science and faith. But before examining the strengths and weaknesses of particular arguments, it is worth pausing a moment and asking why the proportion of scientists who are committed Christians is apparently as high as in the general population.

There is no simple answer to this question. A few years ago I wrote to fourteen leading scientists I knew to be Christians, and asked them to set down the differences their science made to their faith, and their faith to their science. I collected their replies into a book entitled *Real Science, Real Faith* (1991).[1] I expected some clear answers to the problems of relating science and faith, because all the people I approached were professionally successful, and knew that fudging and prevaricating do not work. The reason I chose the individuals I did was not to add one more book of Christian success stories, but to demonstrate that Christians can rise to the top of the scientific tree without in any way compromising their allegiance to Christ. What I did not expect was the great variety of the experiences and 'contexts' of the fourteen respondents. Some described

---

[1] At the same time that *Real Science, Real Faith* was published, Nevill Mott, Nobel Laureate for Physics for his work on the properties of semi-conductors, also produced a collection of essays by scientists called *Can Scientists Believe? Some Examples of the Attitude of Scientists to Religion* (1991). I sent a copy of my book to Mott. He thanked me for it, but said it was 'rather depressing', to him, because of the implicit assumption of its contributors that 'a Christian is necessarily one who looks to the Bible'. This was an interesting and somewhat surprising response, because a scientist is a person who (almost by definition) uses *all* the relevant evidence in his reasoning, even though he or she may (and should) be ruthlessly critical in interpreting that evidence.

their intellectual pilgrimage and the implications of their science for belief; others wrote of their sickness, indecisions and disappointments. But all were explicit that they were where they were because of God's hand on them. Science was a vocation just as strong and real as the occupations we normally think of as vocations (medicine, nursing, teaching, evangelism, pastoral ministry, and so on). The common factor – perhaps the *only* common factor – was the certainty that the God of the Bible both cares and acts, and influences events and people for his own divine purposes. And that is what this book is about.

2

REASON

As God is the God of history and as God has created us in his image, the critical use of all the tools of human reason and study which are required for academic integrity are also required for us for a simple and basic theological reason, the being and giving of God.

David Jenkins (1987:16)

The early scientists (that is, those who lived after the beginnings of 'modern' science in the sixteenth century) were explicit and often devout believers. Johannes Kepler (1571–1630) wrote of 'thinking God's thoughts after him' as he contemplated the stars; Blaise Pascal (1623–62) experienced a profound religious awakening and became a committed Jansenist (these were a group believing in the controlling effects of divine grace); Robert Boyle (1627–91) gave money to make the New Testament available to the native peoples of North America; Isaac Newton (1642–77) devoted himself as much to theology as to physics; and Michael Faraday (1791–1867) observed that the Christian 'finds his guide in the Word of God, and commits the keeping of his soul into the hands of God. He looks for no assurance beyond what the Word can give him, and if his mind is troubled by the cares and fears which assail him he can go nowhere but in prayer to the throne of grace and to Scripture.' Two thirds of the founders of the Royal Society of London in 1663 had strong Puritan leanings.

But as knowledge of science grew, the place for God seemed to grow smaller. The comment of the French astronomer, the Marquis de Laplace (1749–1827), when asked by Napoleon about the place of God in his science, is often quoted: 'Sire, I have no need of that hypothesis.' This was not actually a denial of the existence of God (Laplace was a practising Roman Catholic), but a recognition that there was no place for a sort of treadmill operator in his universe. The older view of life is somewhat imaginatively described by G. M. Trevelyan (1938:53–54):

> The idea of regular law guiding the universe was unfamiliar to the contemporaries of Francis Bacon.[1] The fields around town and hamlet were filled, as soon as the day-labourers had left them, by goblins and will-o'-the-wisps; and the woods, as soon as the forester had closed the door of his hut, became the haunt of fairies; the ghosts could be heard gibbering all night under the yew-tree of the churchyard; the witch, a well-known figure in the village, was in the pay of lovers whose mistresses were hard to win, and of gentleman-farmers whose cattle had sickened. If a criminal was detected and punished, the astonishing event was set down as God's revenge against murder; if a dry summer threatened the harvest, the parson was expected to draw down rain by prayer. The charms that ward off disease, the stars of birth that rule fortune, the comet that foretold the wars in Germany, the mystic laws that govern the fall of the dice, were the common interest of ordinary men and women. In a soil that imagination had so prepared, poetry and Puritanism were likely to flourish loftily among lofty men, basely among the base. The better kind of men were full of ardour, fancy and reverence. The ignoble were superstitious, ignorant and coarse. The world was still a mystery, of which the wonder was not dispelled in foolish minds by a daily stream of facts and cheap explanations.

Science changed this: increasingly modern men and women found themselves in a bigger and bigger cosmos regulated by laws which were being discovered and made known by the 'new philosophers'. It was not necessarily more frightening than the older version, because there were so many unknowns in the ancient form, which had always been explained away (as distinct from being explained). And it was still God's world, designed and made by God. John Ray's *The Wisdom of God Manifested in*

---

[1] Francis Bacon (1561–1626) was an exemplar of the death of scholasticism; he explicitly rejected the deductive logic of Aristotle and the Greeks, and stressed the importance of experiment and inductive reasoning, that is, that humans are the servants and interpreters of nature, that truth is not derived from authority and that knowledge is the fruit of experience.

the Works of Creation (1691) was widely read and regularly reprinted into the nineteenth century.

Such a mechanical idea of the world and its creatures was wholly non-contentious at the time. Science actively promoted the cause of religion by showing the beautiful workmanship of the world. Only a wise and good Creator could have made ducks' feet and bills to be just the shape they would need for their survival. It was a good God who had put the mountains in the right places to precipitate rain from the clouds and give us water to drink. Such was the 'argument from design'; it did a good job in concentrating attention on God's wisdom and workmanship. As scientific knowledge grew, religion became less nervous and super-stitious, more calm and rational. Belief in witchcraft and evil spirits, omens and portents, receded; faith became milder and cooler.

As faith became more rational, miracles and the supernatural became less important. Archdeacon William Paley encapsulated the new approach. His *Natural Theology: Or Evidence of the Existence and Attributes of the Deity Collected from the Appearance of Nature* (1802; extensively plagiarized from John Ray), was one of the more influential books of the early nineteenth century. It begins:

In crossing a heath, suppose I pitched my foot against a stone and were asked how the stone came to be there: I might possibly answer, that, for anything I knew to the contrary, it had lain there for ever; nor would it perhaps be very easy to show the absurdity of this answer. But suppose I found a *watch* upon the ground, and it should be inquired how the watch happened to be in that place; I should hardly think of the answer which I had before given, – that, for anything I knew, the watch might have always been there. Yet why should not this answer serve for the watch as well as for the stone? Why is it not as admissible for the second case, as the first? For this reason, and for no other, viz., that, when we come to inspect the watch, we perceive (what we could not discover in the stone) that its several parts are framed and put together for a purpose, e.g. that they are so formed and adjusted as to produce motion, and that motion so regulated as to point out the hour of the day . . . This mechanism being observed (it requires indeed an examination of the subject, to perceive and understand it; but being once, as we have said, observed and understood), the inference we think is inevitable, that the watch must have had a maker: that there must have existed, at some time, and at some place or other, an artificer or artificers who formed it for the purpose which we find it actually to answer.

Charles Darwin read Paley while he was a student at Cambridge. It delighted him; he learnt passages by heart. He looked at the world through Paley's eyes. Paley argued that each part of an animal's body is useful to it in its way of life, and that this universal adaptation illustrates the wisdom and benevolence of a God who cares for his creatures. Just as the intricate structure of a watch implies a watchmaker, so the incredible complexity of living things proclaims the power of their Designer. Paley's interpretation was followed by the eight Bridgewater Treatises (so-called because their authors received support from the bequest of the Eighth Earl of Bridgewater). The eight authors used various scientific subjects to demonstrate 'the Power, Wisdom, and Goodness of God as manifested in the Creation'. But the final major defence of the old understanding was Philip Gosse's *Omphalos: An Attempt to Untie the Geological Knot* (1857). Gosse was a distinguished naturalist. He was also a member of the Plymouth Brethren. His book discussed whether Adam had a navel (an omphalos). Since he regarded Adam to be a special creation and not the son of a natural mother, Gosse argued there was no anatomical reason why he should have had one. However, he would then have been atypical, and not like all his descendants, so Gosse concluded that God created him with a navel. Using similar logic, Gosse maintained that the Garden of Eden into which God placed Adam would have had trees created in the same week as Adam, but they would be 'as if' they had lived many years. Likewise, God created the rocks with fossils already in them (possibly to confuse 'godless scientists'). To the present-day reader, Gosse's ratiocinations seem gloriously implausible (although most creationists who believe in a strict six-day creation still hold to a very similar 'apparent age' theory), but his logic is impeccable. There is no way of directly refuting his arguments.

But the reconciliation of the developing science of geology with the Bible stories in Genesis produced problems to which there were no easy answers. For example, Thomas Burnet, as early as 1682, calculated in *The Sacred Theory of the Earth* that eight times the volume of water in the present oceans would be needed to cover all the terrestrial areas of earth. Burnet suggested that this water must have come from undersea caverns. Notwithstanding, by the eighteenth century the number of major changes in fossil faunas led to proposals of a whole series of floods; it was becoming as difficult to believe in a single Noah's flood as it was for the medieval astronomers to 'save' Ptolemy's interlocking crystal spheres which were supposed to make up the heavens.

More far-reaching was the growing evidence that the surface of the earth has not always been the same. One of the first pointers was the discovery of extinct volcanoes in central France, which led to the recognition that basalt, a widely distributed rock, is nothing but ancient lava. At about the same time, it was realized that many – indeed, most – geological strata are sedimentary, deposited from water, and sometimes these deposits may be tens of thousands of metres thick. This was extremely disturbing: it must have taken an immense amount of time for such thick strata to be deposited, so the earth might be much older than previously thought. Even worse was the finding that neither the volcanic nor the sedimentary rocks have remained unchanged after being laid down. They were subsequently eroded by water cutting valleys through them, and in many cases sedimentary layers have been folded and occasionally turned over completely at some time after deposition.

All of this stimulated interest in the age of the Earth. Isaac Newton calculated that the Earth must have cooled for at least 50,000 years until it was cool enough for life, but he felt that something must be wrong with his sums because this was so much longer than the church's teaching that creation took place less than 6,000 years previously.

In *Les Epoches de la nature* (1779), the Comte de Buffon (1739–88), Director of the Royal Botanic Garden in Paris, reported on some experiments he had performed, involving heating a group of spheres of various sizes. He concluded that 74,832 years were required for the Earth to cool from white heat to its present condition. (He privately estimated that the Earth was at least half a million years old, but did not publish this figure, because an earlier book of his had been censored.) In an attempt to harmonize his results with Scripture, Buffon argued that there had been seven epochs of Earth history, more or less matching the days of creation in Genesis. In other words, he suggested, his interpretation was not all that different from the traditional one, so long as the Genesis days were taken as 'epochs' rather than twenty-four-hour periods:

1. Formation of earth and planets.
2. Origination of the great mountain ranges.
3. Water covering all dry land.
4. Beginning of volcanic activity.
5. Elephants and other tropical animals inhabiting the north temperate area familiar to Buffon.

6. Separation of continents (Buffon appreciated the similarity of North American animals to those of Europe and Asia, and reasoned that the two land masses must have been connected with each other at some time in the past).

7. Appearance of human beings.

Another problem for the eighteenth-century understanding of the Genesis story was the ever-increasing knowledge of fossils. Fossils were, of course, well known, but for a long time they were believed to be nothing more than an accident of nature (*lusus naturae*) rather than the remains of once living creatures. As time passed, the organic origin of fossils became increasingly accepted. The last capable naturalist to advocate an inorganic origin seems to have been Johann Beringer of the University of Würzburg. Beringer loved to collect and sketch fossils, but was convinced that they were simply curious shapes produced by nature. His *Lithographiae Wirceburgeinsis* (1726) contained drawings and descriptions of all manner of objects dug from local quarries, including many genuine fossils, but also images of birds sitting on their nests, entirely imaginary animals, and Hebrew letters. Such extremely odd discoveries confirmed Beringer in his belief that fossils were not buried organisms, until one day he discovered a rock with his own likeness and name on it. The perpetrators of the hoax, envious of Beringer's reputation, had baked and carved fake fossils and planted them in Beringer's favourite collecting spots. Beringer spent the rest of his life attempting to recall all the published copies of his book.

However, the common explanation for fossils was that they represented creatures drowned in Noah's flood. In very early Christian times Tertullian (160–225) wrote of fossils in mountains as demonstrating a time when the globe was overrun by water, although it is not clear whether or not he was talking about Noah's time. Both Chrysostom and Augustine thought of the flood as being responsible for fossils, and Martin Luther was even more certain. Notwithstanding, there were two problems about the 'flood theory'.

First, unknown and – as the knowledge of living animals and plants increased apace – presumably extinct organisms were found as fossils. The discovery of extinct organisms conflicted not so much with the Bible as with the theologians' 'principle of plenitude', which held that God in the breadth of his mind had surely created any creature that was possible; and conversely God in his benevolence could not possibly permit any of his own creatures to become extinct. Plenitude was usually linked with the idea of a *scala naturae*, that there could be no gaps between forms in the chain. It also commonly involved an assumption of increasing perfection, more 'soul', more consciousness, more ability to reason, or greater advance towards God. Extinctions were a problem for interpretation rather than a true conflict with Scripture.

The second problem arose from information collected by an English surveyor, William Smith, and a French zoologist, Baron Cuvier, which indicated that particular rock strata have distinctive fossils. Smith was involved in canal-building and attempting to trace coal seams in mines, and he realized that geological strata could be identified by the fossils they contained. Such strata can sometimes be followed for hundreds of miles even when the rock formation changes. Smith developed these principles between 1791 and 1799, although his 'stratigraphic map' of England and Wales was not published until 1815. During the same period French naturalists were actively collecting fossils in the limestone quarries around Paris, and Cuvier worked out the exact stratigraphy of these fossils (mainly mammals) in detail. The conclusion – unpalatable as it was at the time – was that there is a time sequence involved in the laying down of fossil-bearing strata, and that the lowest strata are the oldest. Later on it was possible to correlate strata, not only across England or western Europe, but between different parts of the world, if allowance was made for the same kinds of regional differences which exist today in living faunas and floras.

At the end of the eighteenth century most geologists regarded the change between successive strata as the result of multiple catastrophes, the later forms being replacements specially made by the creator. The hangover from Plato's ideas about the impossibility of change prevented the fossil record being interpreted as a sequence of continuing changes, as it would conventionally be seen as today.

The idea of evolution was in the air, as it were, during the second half of the eighteenth century. Maupertuis, Buffon and Diderot (Frenchmen), and Rodig, Herder, Goethe and Kant (Germans) have all been claimed as evolutionists, albeit without general support from historians of science. They all postulated new origins (rather than a change in an existing type) or a simple 'unfolding' of innate potential. Nevertheless, they are significant as being the immediate predecessors of Lamarck, who was the first to make a real break with the old, Plato-dominated worldview.

We shall consider evolution in the next chapter. My purpose here is more restricted: to show that science produced questionings and doubts about the traditional worldview in scholars who believed wholly in the Bible record. At least up to the beginning of the nineteenth century, scientists were just as devout a group as were their non-scientific contemporaries, and saw their pursuit of science as a largely religious activity. Clear summaries of the historical interactions between science and faith are given by Colin Russell in his books *Cross-Currents* (1985) and *The Earth, Humanity and God* (1994), and by John Brooke in *Science and Religion* (1991).

The nature of science

As time passed and scientific knowledge grew, it became apparent that old *assumptions* about the nature of the world were wrong, and that the *interpretations* of the Bible based on these assumptions were often incorrect. It is important to emphasize that we are talking about assumptions and interpretations and not about the nature of reality or the authority of Scripture. The saga of Galileo Galilei (1564–1642) well illustrates both these points.

In his book *De Revolutionibus* (1543), the Polish astronomer Nicholas Copernicus put forward the idea that the Earth and the other planets moved round the Sun, rather than the Earth being the static centre of the system. The reason for this was dissatisfaction with the Ptolemaic system, not experimental evidence. There was no great debate at the time, although some decades later the Reformer Melanchthon objected on the grounds that 'the sun, which is like a bridegroom coming forth . . . rises at one end of the heavens and makes its circuit to the other' (Ps. 19:4–6) and 'You [God] established the earth' (Ps. 119:90). John Calvin rejected a moving Earth on the ground of common sense, not of Scripture. Then in 1610, Galileo reported observations made with his newly invented telescope, which showed that the Earth was indeed in motion. He was condemned on the grounds that Joshua had commanded the sun to stand still (Jos. 10:12) (implying that it normally moves), and it was made clear that the intervention of a layman in matters of theological principle was unwelcome. In 1616 the Congregation of the Index concluded that to teach that the Sun was at the centre of the universe 'expressly contradicts the doctrine of Holy Scripture in many passages'.

Galileo was called to Rome and reminded that Copernican teaching was officially unsanctioned, and that might have been the end of the story. In 1632, however, Galileo published his *Dialogue Concerning the Two Principal Systems of the World*, in which one of the disputants was pictured as a buffoonish and dim champion of orthodoxy, and was clearly a caricature of the pope himself, Urban VIII. Galileo was summoned before the Inquisition and forced to recant. (Rumour has it that on rising from his knees, he said, 'But it [the Earth] does move.')[2]

There can be very few people nowadays who still hold to the idea of a stationary Earth at the heart of the solar system, and examination of the verses in the Psalms shows that they are concerned with the immutability of God, not details of astronomy. As Galileo himself wrote in his *Letter to the Grand Duchess Christina* (1615), the Bible 'teaches us how to go to heaven, not how the heavens go'.

The Vatican revoked its anti-Copernican edict in 1757 and removed Galileo's *Dialogue* from the Index in 1831, but it was not until 1992 that Galileo was formally declared to be right in his dispute with the Inquisition. This conclusion, however, was tempered by the observation that both Galileo and his persecutors acted 'in good faith', and that the Inquisition, faced with the creation account in Genesis on the one hand and Galileo's inference on the other, had no choice but to believe the former. *Nature* commented (360:2, 5 November 1992): 'With the passage of so much time, many will say that this old tale, however heroic, has no present significance. But this would be mistaken. The Galileo business remains a present problem because it provides a perpetual licence for prejudice in the evaluation of discovery . . . the Vatican has not moved much in 359 years.'

The most satisfactory solution to the debate about Galileo and Bible, and to issues of science and faith generally, is to accept that they give complementary accounts of reality. This is implicit in the old idea that God has given us two books, the Bible and the 'book of nature'. Unfortunately these books have too often been read independently of each other. How can they be read together?

Perhaps the simplest way of approaching this is to oversimplify reality and talk of 'How?' and 'Why?' questions. Scientists study *how* things work: what causes plants to grow, animals to mate, minerals to form, and so on. They do this by testing an idea (or *hypothesis*) by means of

---

[2] A readable account of the controversies surrounding Galileo, and their general context, is given by Charles Hummel in *The Galileo Connection: Resolving Conflicts between Science and the Bible* (1986).

experiments or other information (from history, other tested hypotheses, and so on). The more tests a hypothesis survives without being disproved, the more likely it is to be right. This is fine and easy to understand, but as scientific knowledge has advanced it has brought with it a wholly false assumption: that if we know *one* cause of an event we know everything about that event. This assumption is not true. A simple analogy may help: we can describe a painting entirely in terms of the distribution of chemical molecules in two-dimensional space. If we knew enough about pigment chemistry, we could give a complete description of that picture in chemical terms. But we can also give a complete description of the same picture in terms of its design and composition, telling why the artist created it as he did. Both our descriptions refer to the same physical object; each is complete in itself, yet they do not overlap at all. It is obviously inadequate to describe the picture as *nothing but* a collection of spatially ordered chemicals; it is equally untrue to assert that it is *nothing but* an artistic design. Obviously our picture has more than one 'cause'.

The application of complementarity to issues of science and faith has been explored by Michael Polanyi (who has developed the idea of different 'levels' of explanation; *cf.* Polanyi 1969) and particularly by Donald MacKay. The latter extended the concept to dynamic processes. It is worth labouring this because of its conceptual value, and it would be difficult to improve on MacKay's (1960) own words:

An imaginative artist brings into being a world of his own invention. He does it normally by laying down patches of paint on canvas, in a certain spatial order (or disorder!). The *order* which he gives the paint determines the *form* of the world he invents. Imagine now an artist able to bring his world into being, not by laying down paint on canvas, but by producing an extremely rapid succession of sparks of light on the screen of a television tube. (This is in fact the way in which a normal television picture is held in being.) The world he invents is now not static but dynamic, able to change and evolve at his will. Both its form and its laws of change (if any) depend on the way in which he orders the sparks of light in space and time. With one sequence he produces a calm landscape with quietly rolling clouds; with another, we are looking at a vigorous cricket match on a village green. The scene is steady and unchanging just for as long as he wills it so; but if he were to cease his activity, his invented world would not become chaotic; it would simply cease to be.

I do not in fact know anyone with sufficient dexterity to perform such feats at the required speed; but that is beside the point. I have sketched our hypothetical artist at work because I find this process quite a helpful illustration of some of the ways in which the Bible talks about God's activity in physical events.

Suppose, for example, that we are watching a cricket match 'brought into being' and 'held in being' by such an artist. We see the ball hit the wicket and the stumps go flying. The 'cause' of the motion of the stumps, in the ordinary sense, is the impact of the ball. Indeed, for any happening in and of the invented scene, we would normally look for – and expect to find – the 'cause' in some other happenings in and of that scene. Given a sufficiently long and self-consistent sample, we might in fact imagine ourselves developing a complete predicitive *science* of the cricket world displayed before us, abstracting 'laws of motion' sufficient to explain satisfactorily (in a scientific sense) every happening we witness – so long as the artist keeps to the same regular principle in maintaining the cricket scene in being.

Suppose, however, that someone suggests that our scientific explanation of these happenings is 'not the only one', and that all our experience of them owes its existence to the continuing stability of the will of the artist who shapes and 'holds in being' the whole going concern. However odd this may sound at first, it is obvious that in fact he is not advancing a *rival* explanation to the one we have discovered in our 'science' of the cricket field; he has no need to cast doubt on ours in order to make room for his own, since the two are not explanations *in the same sense*. They are answers to different questions, and both may, in fact, be entirely valid.

The parallel I think is clear as far as it goes. The God in whom the Bible invites belief is no 'cosmic mechanic'. Rather is he the Cosmic Artist, the creative Upholder, without whose continual activity there would be not even chaos, but just nothing. What we call physical laws are expressions of the regularity that we find in the pattern of created events that we study as the physical world. Physically, they express the nature of the entities 'held in being' in the pattern. Theologically, they express the stability of the great Artist's creative will. Explanations in terms of scientific laws and in terms of divine activity are thus not rival answers to the same question; yet they are not talking about different things. They are (or at any rate purport to be) complementary accounts of different aspects of the same happening, which in its full nature cannot be adequately described by either alone.

The idea that an event has more than one cause is at least as old as Aristotle, who distinguished material and efficient causes (which answer the question 'How?') from formal and final causes (which answer the question 'Why?'). The fallacy of 'nothing buttery' is to believe that we know everything about an event when we can answer the question 'How?'

The tragedy is that we assume that scientists have excluded God from the world if we can answer 'How?' questions without referring to him; we assume that there is less and less room for God in our world as we know more and more about how it works. God is squeezed into the ever-decreasing gaps in our knowledge. Put another way, since 1543 God has been progressively confined to events we cannot yet explain. The only way to keep such a God in the universe is to make him ever smaller. A few years ago it was fashionable to say that God controlled the position of electrons, which theory (Heisenberg's uncertainty principle) states it is impossible to predict. But this approach is not very convincing: either he is Lord of all, or he is not Lord at all.

The truth is that science is concerned only with 'How?' questions; although it is possible to frame some of these as 'Why?' questions (for example: why are insect-pollinated flowers brightly coloured? Why do herring gulls have red spots on their beaks?), in general they are questions which it is meaningless for a scientist to ask. Sir Peter Medawar, a Nobel Laureate for his work in immunology, has stated the situation clearly:

> That there is indeed a limit upon science is made very likely by the existence of questions that science cannot answer and that no conceivable advances of science would empower it to answer. These are the questions children ask – the ultimate questions of Karl Popper.[3] I have in mind such questions as:
>
> > How did everything begin?
> > What are we all here for?
> > What is the point of living?
>
> Doctrinaire positivism – now something of a period piece – dismissed all such questions as nonquestions or pseudoquestions such as only simpletons ask and charlatans of one kind or another profess to be able to answer. This peremptory dismissal leaves one empty and dissatisfied because the questions make sense to those who ask them, and the answers to those who give them; but whatever else may be in dispute, it would be universally agreed that it is not to science that we should look for answers. There is then a prima-facie

---

[3] Popper (1978:342) commented: 'Science does not make assertions about ultimate questions – about the riddles of existence, or about man's task in this world.'

case for the existence of a limit to scientific understanding (Medawar 1984:66).

The significance of the complementarity approach to causation is that it removes the problems of inevitable determinism expected of events in a mechanical universe. If our thoughts, actions, beliefs and very existence are the unalterable consequence of being part of an enormous cosmic machine, our humanness becomes a mere fiction. This would mean that free will and morality would be an illusion, since they would in principle be foreseeable from a knowledge of the causal events that brought us into being – a chain of cause and effect that could theoretically be traced back to the beginning of time. Much time and effort have been spent in trying to find how to fit God into this seemingly impenetrable machine: the difficulty is that the gaps left for him become ever smaller as we learn more about physical processes, and it is both futile and wholly unconvincing to invent a spiritual world unconnected to the real world of atoms and organisms. That is why complementarity is important, providing as it does a logically coherent and emotionally satisfying account of God and his relation to the world. We need to explore the significance of different levels of explanation and causes of events, rather than blaming science for declining morals and seeking salvation in some form of self-potentiation.[4]

Reductionism

The assumption that science is all-powerful and can answer all questions leads to the notion of reductionism, that is, the belief that all knowledge (and in the context, that means all science) can be reduced to a few simple axioms or processes. Physicists sometimes speak of their search for a 'Grand Unified Theory' or, even more ambitiously, a 'Theory of Everything'. Such a search depends on the assumption that all phenomena are nothing more than the sum of their parts, and that a full knowledge of the properties of the 'parts' will tell us everything about the

---

[4] A diatribe about the dangers of science and scientists by the philosopher Mary Midgley (*Science as Salvation: A Modern Myth and its Meaning*, 1992) is interesting because it largely ignores determinism, which is surely a greater threat to values than inappropriate ethics based on scientific discoveries, since it could imply that we are 'only' animals.

whole. A common counter to this is that it is impossible to predict even the properties of water, a liquid which freezes at 0°C but has its maximum density at 4°C, from the properties of hydrogen and oxygen which are its sole constituents. To say that water is 'nothing but' a combination of two gases is to ignore completely the 'emergent properties' of the compound. Indeed, it is almost a truism to state that the characteristics of a whole organism or organization are greater than the sum of its parts: an animal has functions and abilities above those of its constituent cells, a society behaves differently from its individual members, and so on. Sometimes we may be able to foretell some of the properties of the whole from the parts, but often this is not possible. This debate spills from the philosophical to the moral realm when we discuss the nature of human beings and are faced with the assertion that we are 'nothing but' a machine, a computer, or a programmed genetic reaction (Holder 1993). We shall return to this point when we discuss human life below (p. 76).

But a sceptic may react to this talk of emergent properties and 'nothing buttery' with the claim that reductionism is a necessary part of science, and that science inevitably involves the breaking down of complex traits to simpler components. This is true, but only in a particular sense: we need to distinguish clearly *operational* reductionism, which is necessary in any scientific investigation and involves the conscious selection of supposedly relevant factors (and hence the rejection of others), from *ontological* reductionism, which assumes that any system can be explained wholly by the properties of its components and which consequently ignores emergent properties and variation (Ayala 1974; Peacocke 1986). The distinction between the so-called 'exact sciences' of physics and chemistry and the 'inexact sciences' of biology and psychology is almost always an ontological claim. Carl Pantin (1968) has argued that '*physics and chemistry have been able to become exact and mature just because so much of the wealth of natural phenomena is excluded from their study*' (his italics). He suggests that such sciences should be called 'restricted'.

A further difficulty is that the study of whole systems ('holism') has become somewhat discredited in biology because it has often been associated with claims about unspecific organizing principles, which have been invented to explain stability or complexity (Golley 1993). At this level holism tends to merge into vitalism and away from conventional science. A good example of this is in Jan Christian Smuts's book *Holism and Evolution* (1926) which sought to trace the evolution of mind and value from molecules. Pierre Teilhard de Chardin developed a similar approach, especially in *The Phenomenon of Man* (1959). It should not need saying that holism does not imply or necessarily involve vitalism, but it is often assumed to do so (Berry 1989).

Conclusion

Science in the popular mind is often equated with knowledge. There are valid historical reasons for this, going back to the confusion between knowledge and authority in medieval times, and the distinction made by David Hume in the eighteenth century between what is the case and what ought to be the case. This led Hume to say that 'morality is more properly felt than judged of', and to the development of a public role for reason (which in practice tends to be the scientific method) separately from private or personal thoughts, which were dismissed as subjective.

This tendency was emphasized and formalized between the wars by the positivism of the 'Vienna Circle', which was avowedly atheistic and thus marginalized religion, the traditional source of values. It perhaps reached its apogee in the book *Chance and Necessity* (1970) by the Nobel Laureate Jaques Monod. He wrote that 'Chance *alone* is at the source of every innovation, of all creation in the biosphere. Pure chance, absolutely free but blind, [is] at the very root of the stupendous edifice of evolution' (p. 110), and that 'holists totally lack understanding of scientific method and of the crucial role analysis plays in it' (p. 80). This is not the place to analyse the rise and fall of different philosophical fashions (a detailed response to Monod was given by Donald MacKay in *Science, Chance and Providence*, 1978; an excellent general guide is Roger Trigg's *Rationality and Science*, 1993), but to insist that science as practised by real scientists is a much more complicated and less sterile pursuit than the philosophers would like us to think.[5]

---

[5] John Polkinghorne (1983:11) commented: 'When I read Monod's book I was greatly excited by the scientific picture it presented of how life came to be. As a particle physicist, I found the biochemical details pretty difficult to follow but, assuming them to be correct, they implied that Schrödinger's equation and Maxwell's equations (the fundamental dynamical equations of quantum theory and electromagnetism respectively, which I could literally write down on the back of an envelope) had this astonishing consequence of the emergence of replicating molecules and eventually life. The economy

Some years ago, Peter Medawar (1990a) wrote an essay entitled 'Is the Scientific Paper a Fraud?' He explained that he did not mean 'that the interpretations you find in a scientific paper are wrong or deliberately mistaken [but that] the scientific paper may be a fraud because it misrepresents the process of thought that accompanied or gave rise to the work that is described in the paper'. His argument was that science does not proceed by induction, ordering an array of facts to produce generalization, but rather (following William Whewell and Karl Popper) by a 'hypothetico-deductive approach' in which the consequences of hypotheses are tested by experiment and then modified or rejected as appropriate. The key question is where the hypothesis came from. Medawar believed that 'scientists should not be ashamed to admit, as many of them apparently *are* ashamed to admit, that hypotheses appear in their minds along uncharted byways of thought; that they are imaginative and inspirational in character; that they are indeed adventures of the mind'.

Medawar followed up his original suggestion (which was actually a broadcast talk) by inviting a number of distinguished scientists to describe how they had carried out a favourite piece of research. Their contributions are collected in a book entitled *Experiment* (Edge 1964). It turned out that many of them were, like Archimedes, inspired by taking a bath. The conventional idea of science as a painstaking accumulation of evidence is misleading; the collection and analysis of data are secondary consequences of the primary scientific enterprise, which is the propounding and refining of hypotheses.

It is at this secondary level that fraud usually enters science, although the fraud can be unintentional (and unpremeditated) because the scientist concerned is so convinced of the correctness of his or her hypothesis that the selection of data (or 'results') is biased towards supporting the hypothesis. Isaac Newton was fond of telling how he was led to propose gravity by an apple falling on his head, but historians tell us he was still

---

and profundity of that is breathtaking. For me, the beauty that is revealed in the structure of the world was like a rehabilitation of the argument from design – not as a knockdown argument for the existence of God (there are no such arguments; nor are there for his non-existence) but as an insight into the way the world is. It is clear that the different reactions of Monod and someone like myself to the same set of scientific facts must arise from something outside the strictly scientific world view itself.

persuaded of the alternative explanation based on Descartes's vortices at the time of his life when the apple was supposed to have dropped on him.

Research is not a wholly rational and explicitly logical procedure, but one subject to the same confinements and constraints that afflict other honest men and women trying to make their way in the world. Medawar (1990b) comments:

> What lesson should the scientific profession learn? Should we go around on our guard, doubting and questioning, looking for fraud and misrepresentation with the air of men expecting to find evidence of it? No, indeed not. Listening for a second time to Sir Kenneth Clark's splendid series of television broadcasts on 'Civilisation', I was again struck by the importance that Clark attached to confidence as a bonding agent in the advance of civilization, as it is indeed throughout professional life. Do not lawyers, bankers, clergymen, librarians, and editors tend to believe their fellow professional unless they have a very good reason to do otherwise? Scientists are the same. The critical scrutiny of all scientific findings – perhaps especially one's own – is an unqualified desideratum of scientific progress. Without it science would surely founder – though not more rapidly, perhaps, than it would if the great collaborative expertise of science were to be subjected to an atmosphere of wary and suspicious disbelief.

Paul exhorted believers to put away falsehood and speak the truth with their neighbours (Eph. 4:25; Col. 3:9). This is a general charge, but it applies to science and scientists especially, since science is concerned with what is, not what ought to be.

3

EVOLUTION AND PURPOSE

I have already quoted four Nobel Prize winners. Here is another one. George Porter, who was awarded the Prize for Chemistry in 1967, wrote in *The Times* of London (21 June 1975) when the nihilism of Jacques Monod was fresh in people's minds:

> Most of our anxieties, problems and unhappiness stem from a lack of purpose which was rare a century ago and which can fairly be blamed on the consequences of scientific enquiry . . . There is one great purpose for man and for us today, and that is to try to discover man's purpose by every means in our power. That is the ultimate relevance of science, and not only science, but of every branch of learning which can improve our understanding. In the words of Tolstoy, 'The highest wisdom has but one science, the science of the whole, the science explaining the Creation and man's place in it.'

The 'scientific enquiry' to which Porter refers is, of course, the implications of the general acceptance of evolution in the nineteenth century and the dethroning of human beings from their assumed position as the crown of creation. If we are nothing but naked apes, we can claim no privileges and no hope beyond that of any other higher animal.

But there is an important qualification: are we 'nothing but' naked apes or are we more than that? Is there any evidence that we are qualitatively different from the other apes?

Genetically we are closely related to the chimpanzees. Jared Diamond, Professor of Physiology at the University of California, Los Angeles, has published a book on *The Rise and Fall of the Third Chimpanzee* (1991), in which he pointed out that there are only two living chimpanzee species commonly recognized, the common chimp (*Pan troglodytes*) and the pygmy chimp (*P. paniscus*). However, if one extracts chimp and human DNA and separates the two strands of the double helix, and then pairs common with pygmy chimp DNA, and chimp with human DNA, only 0.7% of the DNA from the two chimp species fails to pair (that is, 99.3% of the genetic material is the same in each species), but also only 1.6% human DNA fails to pair with chimp. In other words, we share the vast majority of our genes with the two chimps. Our next closest relative is the gorilla, from whom we differ in 2.3% of our DNA.

Diamond argues that this closeness of genetic material means that we ought to be in the same genus as the other chimpanzees; we should be called *Pan sapiens*, or perhaps they should be *Homo troglodytes* and *H. paniscus*. We are more like the chimps than (say) the two gibbon species are to each other (they differ at 2.2% of their DNA) or willow warblers and chiff-chaffs (bird species very difficult to tell apart; they differ by 2.6%). He does not propose that we should be reclassified; he discusses at some length why we are so different from our close genetic relatives. (His solution is that the anatomy of our larynx enabled us to develop speech and thence social organization in ways not open to our 'relatives'.) His problem is why we have risen so far only to fall again by greed, overpopulation and irresponsibility.

It is not my purpose to follow Diamond's thesis in detail. My point is simply that we are genetically a close kin of the great apes, a group of rather generalized primates found mostly in tropical forests.

Diamond is only the latest in a long line of biologists to ponder on the similarities between the human and other species. For example, we have forty-six chromosomes compared with forty-eight in the other primates, but the difference is merely due to two ape acrocentric chromosomes fusing to form a single metacentric one (Robertsonian translocation). The structure and banding of the chromosomes are otherwise very similar. Many genes are linked together in the same order on chromosome segments, even in species as distinct as human and house mouse. Many proteins show only minor differences in amino acid composition from those in other mammal species, and there are, in general, more differences between distantly related forms (such as between bats and elephants) than closely related ones. Many of the differences between apes and humans can be attributed to changes in growth and maturation rates; in some ways we can be regarded as sexually mature embryonic apes (that is, our development has been much slower than in other apes) (De Beer 1940). Biologically we are apes, and the obvious inference is that we are close relatives of some of them.

The human fossil record continues to be controversial, and has had its share of irrelevancies such as the Piltdown forgery. Notwithstanding, *Homo sapiens* has a more complete fossil history than most species, and one where the fossil findings parallel the genetic ones, that is, an origin in Africa, followed by colonization of most temperate parts of the world. There is dispute about the precise lineages, but general agreement among dispassionate observers of the pattern of spread.

All these lines of evidence point to the animal relationships of humankind. I believe this is inescapable. I also believe it is scriptural: the first creation account in Genesis tells us that we were created on the same day as the other animals, and were distinguished from them by 'God's image'. The second account says that the distinction between humankind and previously created material was God's spirit or breath. Calvin commented on Genesis 2:7 that 'man is linked with the natural creation' by the fact that his body is made of the same substance as the rest of creation, and distinguished through being 'endued with a soul, whence it received vital motion; and on the soul he engraved his own image to which immortality is annexed'. In other words, we are a special creation in our humanness, and this humanness is not located in any specific physical part of us.

I will return to these points later; a proper understanding of our true humanness is crucial to how we treat our neighbours. But I digress first to discuss the general topic of evolution, which is the first of my case-studies of the action of God in the world. My thesis is that we do not have to choose between the conclusions of science (evolution) and the Bible record; both are true and complement each other (Kitcher 1982; Van Till *et al.* 1990). To force a choice between evolution and Scripture is as false as the choice imposed by the pope on Galileo (pp. 18–19).

Lamarck and Darwin

Jean-Baptiste Lamarck (1744–1829) was a protégé of Buffon, and from 1788 until his death worked in the French Natural History Museum. His key work was an evolutionary *Philosophie zoologique* (1809), which he stated was needed to explain two phenomena: (1) the gradual increase in 'perfection' from the simplest animals to man, seen simply in terms of complexity; and (2) the amazing diversity of organisms.

On these grounds, Lamarck claimed that one species may, over a long period of time, become 'transformed' into a new species; such evolutionary change solves the problem of extinctions. The snag is that in solving one difficulty, Lamarck produced a greater one. 'Transformism' introduces a time factor, which has been described as the Achilles' heel of natural theology: although a creator could design a perfect organism in an unchanging world, this would be impossible if the environment was changing. Adaptation to changes to climate, to the physical structure of the earth's surface, and of predators and competitors is possible only if organisms can adjust to their circumstances; in other words, if they evolve.

This idea that change could take place over time was the important contribution of Lamarck. Scientifically his ideas had little credence outside his native France; although he prepared the way for Darwin in pointing to evidence that evolutionary change must have occurred, it is not true to claim that the two men's approaches or contributions were similar. Fifty years after Lamarck, Darwin wrote that the *Philosophie zoologique* was 'veritable rubbish . . . I got not a fact or idea from it'. I have already suggested that the simple idea that the earth was no more than a few thousand years old was becoming difficult to maintain before the end of the eighteenth century (p. 15), although the traditional date of 4004 BC[1] was probably still assumed by most people. But increasingly, the date of creation was being pushed back in time (Young 1982).

In 1830, Charles Lyell published the first volume of his *Principles of*

[1] There are still Bibles which head the marginal notes of the first chapter of Genesis with the date 4004 BC. This timing was calculated by Archbishop Ussher of Armagh (who rather appropriately was also Professor of Theological Controversies at Trinity College, Dublin) in a book (*Annals of the Ancient and New Testaments*) published in 1650, by the simple method of adding up the ages of all the people in the biblical genealogies from Adam to Christ. John Lightfoot, Vice-Chancellor of Cambridge University and a contemporary of Ussher's, went further, and deduced that creation was completed at 9.00am on Sunday 23 October. Ussher's arithmetic is perfectly sound (add up the ages of the patriarchs given in Gn. 5, 11 and 19, and you get a figure of 2,046 years from the creation of Adam to the age of Abraham at the time of the birth of Isaac. The time of Abraham can be dated from several independent archaeological sources: according to the *New Bible Dictionary* it was around 2000 to 1850 BC). The difficulty is that it places Adam as living at a time when there was already considerable urban civilization in the Middle East, thus lessening his claim to be the genetic founder of the whole human race.

Geology, a book which had a great influence on Darwin. For Lyell, all geological processes were the results of secondary causes, that is, they did not require supernatural interventions. He was a 'uniformitarian' in contrast to the prevailing 'catastrophism', whose subscribers assumed that God must have repeatedly created new species following the recurrent catastrophes revealed in the fossil record. For most of his life Lyell was a firm opponent of evolution, although he was ultimately persuaded by Darwin.

Then in 1844 a book was published in London which blasted the genteel debates of the time. It sold more than twice as many copies in the ten years after its publication as either Lyell's *Principles* or Darwin's *The Origin of Species. The Vestiges of the Natural History of Creation* was so challenging to contemporary attitudes that the author took every precaution to remain anonymous; speculations about his identity ranged from Lyell and Darwin to Queen Victoria's husband, Prince Albert. Adam Sedgwick, Professor of Geology at Cambridge and Darwin's teacher, exploded with a review that stretched to eighty-five pages. He wrote to Lyell: 'If the book is true, the labours of sober induction are in vain; religion is a lie, human law is a mass of folly, and a base injustice; morality is a moonshine; our labours for the black of Africa were works of madmen; and man and woman are only better beasts.'

The author of the *Vestiges* was Robert Chambers, although this became known only after his death in 1871. He was a popular essayist, and editor of the *Chambers Encyclopaedia*. He took an avowedly Christian stance, believing that when there is a choice between special creation and the operation of general laws instituted by the Creator, 'the latter is greatly preferable as it implies a far grander view of the divine power and dignity than the other'. He had no doubt that the available fossil evidence showed that the fauna of the world had evolved through geological time, and, since there is nothing in inorganic nature 'which may not be accounted for by the agency of the ordinary forces of nature', why not consider 'the possibility of plants and animals having likewise been produced in a natural way'?

What Chambers did was consistently to apply uniformitarianism to organic nature. The hierarchy of animals was meaningless to him unless one adopted evolution. Like Darwin, he constantly emphasized how many phenomena, for instance rudimentary organs, could be explained as the product of evolution, although this made no sense in terms of special creation.

Chambers made many errors. Darwin described his book: 'The prose is perfect, but the geology strikes me as bad and his zoology far worse.' Chambers advocated no real mechanism by which change could occur. But he convinced some influential people, including A. R. Wallace, the philosophers Herbert Spencer and Arthur Schopenhauer, and the poet Ralph Waldo Emerson. More importantly, he accustomed people to the idea of evolution; Darwin wrote that he did 'excellent service in calling in this country attention to the subject'. The critics of the *Vestiges* supplied the standard objections to evolution, which Darwin took care to answer in the *Origin*.

Darwin (1809–82)

And so we come to Charles Darwin, younger son of a country doctor and one-time intending ordinand. It was his book *The Origin of Species by Means of Natural Selection, or the preservation of favoured races in the struggle for life* (first published 1859, sixth and final edition 1872) that led to the general acceptance of evolutionary ideas in both the scientific and the general world. The reason for the immediate success of the *Origin* was Darwin's explanations for the distribution of animals and plants, and his convincing interpretation of the significance of vestigial organs. Other lines of evidence, from fossils, anatomical likenesses, and so on, were well known to Darwin's contemporaries but were explained away by them because they did not understand how evolution could work. Indeed, it was Darwin's easily understood *mechanism* of evolution which was his most important contribution. The need for a mechanism before a scientific idea is generally accepted has a parallel with the hypothesis of continental drift, which was put forward in detail by Wegener in 1915, but not commonly accepted until the nature and behaviour of tectonic plates were described by geophysicists in the 1960s.

Darwin's original intention was to write a definitive book on evolution, what he called his 'Big Book'. In the spring of 1858, however, he was sent by Alfred Russel Wallace an essay, *On the Tendency of Varieties to Depart Indefinitely from the Original Type*, written in the Moluccas by Wallace while recovering from fever and which set out the same mechanism for organic change which Darwin had been working on for almost twenty years. Darwin felt that Wallace's letter should be published, but on the urging of his friends Charles Lyell (whose *Principles* had first alerted Darwin to the reality of long-continued gradual geological change) and J. D. Hooker (son of the effective founder of Kew Botanical Gardens, and instigator of the study of plant geography), he allowed a revised version of an essay he had written fifteen years previously to be forwarded with it to the Linnean Society. The two papers were read at a meeting of the Society on 1 July 1858. Both papers contain the three facts and two conclusions which are commonly taken as the simple summary of Darwinian evolution: the potential of all species to increase greatly in numbers, coupled with an approximate constancy in numbers, implies that there is a struggle for existence; and when variation is added to this, it becomes clear that natural selection must operate.

It was the ease with which these propositions could be understood that helped the fact of evolution to be generally accepted. In fact Darwin devoted more than half of the *Origin* to different lines of evidence that evolution had occurred: he had two chapters on the fossil record, two on geographical distributions, and one each on morphological likenesses (including comparative embryology, the interpretation of vestigial organs, and the meaning of classification), behaviour, and domestication. He devoted later books specifically to sexual selection and the origin of man, domestication, and adaptations in plants for pollination, insect-eating, and climbing. All these were parts of the 'Big Book' Darwin had originally intended to write before being forced into print by Wallace.

In chapters 6 and 7 of the *Origin* Darwin dealt with 'difficulties' and 'miscellaneous objections' to his theory. His main points concerned the nature of species and questions about the efficacy of selection. In a later chapter, he discussed the imperfections of the fossil record. Darwin knew that the maintenance of variation was a key weakness in his theory. The causes of variation are repeatedly referred to in the book, and in later editions of the *Origin* he tended to accept that some Lamarckian explanation might be necessary (that is, that the heredity of an individual might be affected by an environmental modification of its body [phenotype]. No claim of Lamarckian inheritance by Kammerer, Lysenko, Steele and many others over the years has ever been substantiated). The problem was not resolved until the physical basis of heredity was discovered following the embryological conclusions of Weissman (1883) and the rediscovery of Mendel's work in 1900.

The furore following the publication of the *Origin* had more or less died down ten years later. In 1882 Darwin died and was buried in Westminster Abbey. The Christian establishment gave a further *imprimatur* when in 1884 Frederick Temple (later to become Archbishop of Canterbury) gave a series of lectures on the relations between religion and science, and argued that Darwin gave paradoxical support for the traditional argument from design for the existence of God: 'God did not make the things, we may say; no, but he made them make themselves.'

Although there were exceptions, it was among orthodox believers with a firm hold on Calvin's doctrine of providence that the least nervousness about Darwinism was experienced (Livingstone 1987). In the United States, three scientists who were evangelicals (James Dana, Asa Gray and George F. Wright) ensured that Darwin's ideas had a fair hearing; in denominational journals George Macloskie, a Presbyterian, and Alexander Winchell, a Methodist, argued their understanding of God and evolution; and distinguished evangelical theologians such as Warfield, Orr, A. A. Hodge, Iverach, Strong, Pope and McCosh all embraced the new biology.

Subsequent decades have seen considerable scientific debate about evolution, as is proper for any scientific theory. These debates, however, have all been about the relative importance of different mechanisms of genetic change, not about the fact of evolution itself (Berry 1982; Mayr 1991). We still talk about the 'theory' of evolution, but we should not be confused by this. The word 'theory' is used in a technical sense by scientists. They distinguish between a set of ideas which are put forward for test, which they call an 'hypothesis', and the accumulated synthesis of tested hypotheses, which is a scientific 'theory'. A theory in scientific language is an established interpretation of facts, and is thus quite different from the speculative rationalizations which are called theories in detective novels. A valuable theory combines a host of observations and conclusions into a single whole (and is sometimes called a *paradigm*), and may incorporate some apparent anomalies which are tolerated for the sake of the synthesis (just as physicists accepted Newtonian mechanics although the orbit of Mercury never fitted the predictions); and suggests experiments and tests for further research. The accusation by some critics that evolution is *only* a theory betrays an ignorance of scientific language; when a biologist talks about evolutionary *theory*, he is referring to a corpus of ideas as firmly grounded as any other in his field.

The most unfortunate hangover from the scientific debates has been a historical myth. Three standard and still-read (or plagiarized) histories of biology (by Nordenskiold, Radl and Singer) were written at a time before the neo-Darwinian synthesis of the late 1930s was established, and when the role of natural selection was thought to be relatively unimportant in evolution. This has meant that non-scientific critics still misjudge the importance and influence of Darwin's own contributions to biology.

We need to insist on what is certain and what is not. The distinguished Harvard geneticist Dick Lewontin is emphatic:

> It is time for students of the evolutionary process, especially those who have been misquoted and used by the creationists, to state clearly that evolution is a *fact*, not theory, and that what is at issue within biology are questions of details of the process and the relative importance of different mechanisms for evolution. It is a *fact* that the earth, with liquid water, is more than 3.6 billion years old. It is a *fact* that cellular life has been around for at least half of that period and that organised multicellular life is at least 800 million years old. It is a *fact* that major forms of the past are no longer living. There used to be dinosaurs and *Pithecanthropus*, and there are none now. It is a *fact* that all living forms come from previous living forms. Therefore, all present forms of life arose from ancestral forms which were different. Birds arose from nonbirds and humans from nonhumans. No person who pretends to any understanding of the natural world can deny these facts any more that she or he can deny that the earth is round, rotates on its axis, and revolves round the sun. (See also Futuyma 1983; Godfrey 1983.)

Apes versus Genesis

The one bit of Darwinian history that almost everyone knows is the confrontation between Bishop Samuel Wilberforce and Thomas Henry Huxley at the 1860 British Association for the Advancement of Science meeting in Oxford. It is unfortunate that Wilberforce was a Christian and Huxley was not, because the evolution debate became a religion *versus* science argument from that moment on, whereas the British Association meeting really showed the death-throes of an outmoded understanding of the world, rather incidentally supported by some bad theology.

Wilberforce had been briefed on the scientific issues of Darwinism by Richard Owen, Director of the Natural History Museum in London. But his main worries were ecclesiastical, and he was concerned to stamp as hard as possible on anything that legitimized change – as, of course, did evolution. His concerns were, first, *sociological*: the conventional church-going population was being disrupted by the movement of people into towns as the Industrial Revolution gathered pace, and there they were less likely to be worshippers. Secondly, they were *theological*: the triumphal progress of manufacture, engineering and colonialism contrasted and apparently conflicted with the Bible's picture of human weakness and the need for redemption. His third area of concern was *ecclesiological*: questionings of the authority of the Bible (and hence of the church) were beginning to spread, fuelled by the 'higher criticism' of German scholars; *Essays and Reviews*, a collection of essays by authors who rejected the verbal inspiration of Scripture, was published in 1860. Wilberforce's attack on evolution was secondary to his main aim of protecting the *status quo* of society and church.

Likewise, Huxley's target was not Christianity but what he regarded as the illegitimate authority of church leaders, holding on to offices of secular power and thus excluding the voice of science, which to Huxley represented objective truth as opposed to superstition. His object was (and remained throughout his life) the secularization of society (Desmond 1994).

There are no verbatim reports of the meeting. Huxley was certain that he had 'won' and that he was 'the most popular man in Oxford for full four & twenty hours afterward'. In contrast, Wilberforce went away happy that he had given Huxley a bloody nose. As far as the audience was concerned, many scored it as an entertaining draw (Desmond & Moore 1991:497). The tragedy has been a legacy of inevitable conflict between science and faith, a conflict encouraged by Huxley himself[2] and fuelled by two much-read manifestos (*History of the Conflict between Religion and Science* by W. Draper, 1875; and *A History of the Warfare of Science with Theology* by A. D. White, 1886). Their influence still persists, even though 'today the views of Draper and White are totally unacceptable, not merely because of many factual aberrations, but much more because they represent a long-demolished tradition of positivist, Whiggish historiography. They wrote from the New World their chronicles of war at a time when science seemed triumphant at home and abroad, and each had his particular reasons for settling old scores with organized religion' (Russell 1989). I believe as a Christian, as a scientist, and as a human being that the most profitable way to deal with disagreement is to

---

[2] He wrote: 'Extinguished theologians lie about the cradle of every science as the strangled snakes besides that of Hercules; and history records that whenever science and orthodoxy have been fairly opposed, the latter has been forced to retire from the lists, bleeding and crushed if not annihilated; scotched if not slain' (*Collected Essays* 2, p. 52. Macmillan, 1893).

identify points of agreement and of dispute, and to analyse the source and importance of the latter. War may be exhilarating, but it should be no more than a prelude to peace.

What do the Genesis accounts of creation actually say, as opposed to what we assume they say?[3] Most importantly, they are about the Creator first and foremost; they are only secondarily about his action. It is God who speaks; it is God who sees his work is good; and it is God who puts his image into humankind. The author of Revelation sums up the position from the other end, as it were, of the Bible:

> You are worthy, our Lord and God,
>   to receive glory and honour and power,
> for you created all things,
>   and by your will they were created and have their being.
>
> (Rev. 4:11)

The Westminster Confession makes the same point: 'God created the world 'for the manifestation of the glory of his eternal power, wisdom and goodness.' Calvin described creation as 'the theatre of [God's] glory'.

Creation was not necessary. God did not 'have to' create the world. 'The God who made the world and everything in it . . . . does not live in temples built by hands. And he is not served by human hands, as if he needed anything, because he himself gives all men life and breath and everything else' (Acts 17:24–25). Both the world and human beings originate from the free and sovereign will of God. From the point of view of creation, the Creator is in every respect independent of his creatures. This distinguishes the Creator of the Bible completely from any pantheistic ideas which say that the living world represents parts or expressions of God, for 'from him and through him and to him are all things' (Rom. 11:36).

The first three chapters of Genesis set the scene for the rest of the Bible, teaching about the nature of God and the impact of evil on the creation. We are presented with the outline of a great range of divine truths – about relationships with God and with each other, and about responsible behaviour. In theological language, Genesis 1 – 3 is a 'theodicy', stating and justifying God's goodness in an evil world. These are all basic facts.

[3] For much of the following paragraphs I am indebted to McKay (1982:245–248), from which quotations (unless otherwise stated) are taken.

The problem we have to face is how to translate the language of these chapters for the 1990s: are we faced with a literal description of God walking around on earth, and the devil in the form of a talking snake; or ought we to take into account other knowledge we have about the world and ourselves? This means that we have to be extremely careful about our *interpretation* of these chapters; our prime concern must be what God is trying to say to us.

The two accounts of creation in Genesis 1 and 2 are complementary. Whatever their literary history, in both there is one supreme God, by whose act and word order was established out of chaos, and upon whom humanity is dependent for its existence and place in the order of created beings; both emphasize obedience to God and fellowship with him; and both introduce ideas integral to the whole of the Old Testament. In his Tyndale Commentary, Kidner (1967) underlines this: in chapters 2 and 3

. . . man is the pivot of the story [while] in chapter 1 he was the climax. Everything is told in terms of him; even the primeval waste is shown awaiting him (2:5b) and the narrative works outwards from man himself to man's environment (gardens, trees, rivers, beasts and birds) in logical as against chronological order, to reveal the world as we are meant to see it: a place expressly designed for our delight and discipline. It is misleading to call this a second creation account, for it hastens to localize the scene, passing straight from the world at large to 'a garden in the east'; all that follows is played out on this narrow stage.

The other general point to make about the biblical Creator is that he is distinct from those portrayed in other middle-eastern mythologies. In the first place, he is presented as a living God, unmistakably personal. The verbs of Genesis 1 express an energy of mind, will and judgment which excludes all question of God being 'it' rather than 'thou'. Secondly, he is the only God, the creator and sovereign of all that is. The world is separate from him, not an emanation or expression. A Jesuit writer, Robert Faricy (1982:2–3), expresses this as the 'dedivinization' of nature:

Genesis underlines that creatures are in no way divine . . . They are merely creatures, not divine, infinitely distant from their ineffably transcendent Creator, and completely subject to him as their Lord . . . Behind the earth's fertility, and causing it, we do not find the sun or the moon, or, as in many myths, the tree of life. We find only the creative word of God. Nature is radically distinct from God.

Thirdly, his ways are perfect. The series of explosions and cataclysms in Genesis declares that heaven can make no truce with sin, whether it is the Godward sin of unbelief and presumption (as in Eden and Babel), or the humanward wrongs of violence, lust and treachery. The Bible God is utterly different from the creator in other widespread myths. There is an Egyptian account dated *c.* 2350 BC which 'describes the act of the god Atum who brought forth gods on a primeval hill above the waters of Chaos. Atum, "who came into being by himself", next brought the world into order and out of the dark deep assigned places and functions to the other deities'. Another myth describes humankind as being created from the tears of the sungod Ra, all people 'being created equal in opportunity to enjoy the basis necessities of life'. However, 'the best known of the Babylonian creation-myths is the adaptation of the Sumerian cosmogony' known as *Enuma Elish*. This begins with two gods, Tiamat and Apsu, but then 'other gods were born [and] Apsu tried to do away with them because of their noise'. But one of them, Ea, managed to kill Apsu; 'then Tiamat, bent on revenge, was herself killed by Ea's son Marduk . . . Marduk used the two halves of Tiamat to create the firmament of heaven and earth. He then set in order the stars, sun and moon, and lastly . . . with the help of Ea, created mankind from the clay mingled with the blood of Kingu, the rebel god who had left Tiamat's forces.

'Throughout the ancient Near East there was a conception of a primary watery emptiness . . . and darkness', with creation 'a divine act *ex nihilo*' (out of nothing) and humans 'made . . . for the service of the gods'. But the Old Testament account stands distinct with its 'clarity and monotheism; there are no struggles between deities or attempts to exalt any special city or race'. The contrasts between Genesis 1 and all the known extrabiblical cosmogonies are more striking than the resemblances.

Turning to the Bible accounts of creation themselves, we should note two points. First, they should not be read as *scientific* accounts. They are concerned with theological truths. This is not to impute factual inaccuracy, but to insist upon the primary purpose of the passages. Just as we speak of 'sunset' rather than saying that 'we can no longer see the Sun from our position on the Earth, because the rotation of the planet has rendered the Sun invisible to us', so we should accept that the Bible uses 'phenomenalistic' language. A moment's reflection shows that this is essential if the Bible is to be understood by all people at all times; scientific language is a very recent and geographically limited invention.

Francis Schaeffer (1973:35–36) has warned:

> We must remember the purpose of the Bible: it is God's message to fallen men . . . The Bible is *not* a scientific textbook if by that one means that its purpose is to give us exhaustive truth or that scientific fact is its central theme and purpose. Therefore, we must be careful when we say we know the flow of history: we must not claim, on the one hand, that science is unnecessary or meaningless, nor, on the other hand, that the extensions we make from Scripture are absolutely accurate or that these extensions have the same validity as the statement of Scripture itself.

Douglas Spanner (1965) has summarized the Bible teaching by saying that it was

> . . . not that God made an elegant mechanism (like a super-clock) and then retired to a distance to watch it perform according to built-in laws; but rather that he remains immanent in His creation, personally energising on a moment-to-moment basis all its multifarious happenings. He 'makes grass grow' (Psalm 104:14), 'makes the hinds to calve' (Psalm 29:9), and 'sends rain' (Matthew 5:45) (note the present tenses). It is in this way that the Bible accounts for the regularity of nature, which we loosely express by saying that similar causes always produce similar effects. This regularity is not due to the perfection of a mechanism, but to the faithfulness of God.

Secondly, both accounts give a clear description of progress, most obviously in Genesis 1 where we begin with chaos and travel through to humankind (the Bible as a whole begins in a garden and ends in a city).

The Genesis 1 progress is interrupted in two ways. First, it describes God's work as taking place in six days. Traditionally the 'days of creation' were taken as literal twenty-four-hour periods, but there are other possible interpretations.

(1) They may represent long periods of time, perhaps geological epochs. This has been a common understanding from the earliest days of the church. Both Origen and Augustine argued that the Genesis 'days' can have no relationship to human days.

(2) The Scottish divine, Thomas Chalmers, suggested that the six days were days of reconstruction, not of creation. He argued that a catastrophe happened between the creation of the heavens and the earth (Gn. 1:1) and the formless and empty earth described in Genesis 1:2. Indeed, there could have been several catastrophes, corresponding to the mass extinctions revealed in the fossil record. The days of reconstruction would have no connection with either the original creation or the fossil record, and therefore (it is argued) there can be no conflict with science. This 'gap theory' was incorporated by Scofield into his 'annotated Bible' and achieved wide circulation among evangelicals. It is, however, exegetically unsound. It depends on reading Genesis 1:2 as 'the earth *became*', which is inadmissible. Also, it requires the verb translated 'make' in Genesis 1 (and Gn. 2:2; Ex. 20:11) to have the meaning 'remake'. There is no justification at all for this.

(3) Philip Wiseman (1948) has argued strongly that, since 'the Sabbath was made for man' (Mk. 2:27; clearly the Creator did not need a day's rest), it was intended for human rest, and so 'it is only reasonable to suppose that what was done on the "six days" also had to do with man; and if with man, then obviously on the six days God was not creating the earth and all life, because man was not in the world when these were being created'. Wiseman then goes on to suggest that the implication of the repeated phrase 'God said' was that God said *to man* what he had done in times past; the six days of Genesis 1 therefore become 'days of revelation'. Like the 'gap theory', however, the idea has exegetical problems because the word translated 'made' in Exodus 20:11 cannot mean 'made known'.

(4) Finally, Genesis 1 may be an ancient hymn. Augustine held this view. There are two triads of days, with similarities between days 1 and 4, 2 and 5, and 3 and 6. Corresponding to light in day 1 are the luminaries of day 4; the creation of the expanse of the sky and the separation of the waters (day 2) correspond to the birds and fish (day 5); and the appearance of dry land and vegetation (day 3) correspond to the land animals, together with the gift of food (day 6). Medieval tradition distinguished the work of separation (days 1–3) from the work of adornment (days 4–6).

All these interpretations are possible (albeit with some problems, as we have recognized). What is important is that they are *interpretations*, and any of them is defensible. It is wrong to be dogmatic. Personally I favour the last of the possibilities, on the ground that God 'rested' on the seventh day. Since we have a God who will never 'slumber nor sleep' (Ps. 121:4), I believe that one of the prime purposes of Genesis 1 is to teach us about the rhythms and disciplines of the week.

The second interruption of progress in Genesis 1 is not apparent in our English translations. The usual word for 'create' is *yâṣar*, which has the sense of 'modelling from pre-existing material', as a potter models or moulds clay (as in Je. 18:3–6). However, another word, *bārā'*, is used in Genesis 1 to describe the origin of matter (verse 1), animal life (verse 21) and human beings (verse 27). In the Old Testament, God is invariably the subject of *bārā'* (e.g. Is. 40:26; 45:7, 8); it emphasizes a special divine action, in contrast to the 'modelling' implied by *yâṣar*. Hence it seems legitimate to suggest that God created in a distinct way when he made matter, animal life, and humankind. All creation is divine activity, but these events seem to have been occasions for some sort of 'special creation' as opposed to 'divine creation through natural processes'.

This leads naturally to the key question of what process(es) God used in creation. Here we have a problem and a paradox in that his mechanisms are not described in the Bible. We are merely told repeatedly that 'God said . . . And it was so'.

God in creation

There are those who assume that if we know the cause of an event, then God cannot be involved. A moment's reflection shows that this cannot be so, or God would be removed from a vast range of processes which we regard as in his providential care. It is better to enquire about what we mean by the 'cause' of an event. As we saw in the last chapter (p. 22), there is nothing inconsistent with knowing the scientific (or material) cause of an event and acknowledging that God is also the (formal) cause of that event. Indeed the author of the book of Hebrews seems to imply that this is how we should approach creation, since 'by faith we understand that the universe was formed at God's command, so that what is seen was not made out of what was visible' (Heb. 11:3). Since it is possible to discover a great deal about the scientific mechanisms through which change has occurred, this can only mean that our acceptance of *God's* creating work is inevitably and properly 'by faith'. It is wholly consistent with both science and Scripture to insist that God is the Creator, but also that he worked through mechanisms which we may discover through scientific research. Like Kepler, the evolutionary geologist or biologist may be 'thinking God's thoughts after him' (see p. 11).

We have already seen how a complementary approach to causation is logically and scientifically appropriate (pp. 20–21), but it is worth returning to the point and emphasizing that knowledge of the cause of a process does not exclude God from that process. Indeed, Scripture only rarely indicates the method God used to achieve his purpose. One such occasion is recorded in Exodus 14:21–22, where we read that 'all that night the LORD drove the sea back with a strong east wind and turned it into dry land. The waters were divided, and the Israelites went through the sea on dry ground . . .' The actual site of the Israelite crossing is uncertain, but at the traditional place, near the northern end of the Gulf of Suez, the water has been blown 'back' several times in recorded history. The prevailing wind in Egypt is from the west, and an east wind is very unusual. Thus God's intervention in this case, although certainly providential, was through natural processes. Notwithstanding, it was truly a miracle. It involved a disturbance of the normal pattern of events by God in such a way as to draw attention to himself; the miracle lay in the place and timing of a physical event, not merely in the fact of its occurrence.

The mechanisms producing the plagues of Egypt are not given in the Bible, but all of them could have perfectly reasonable natural causes: deposits from upstream lakes not infrequently stain the Nile flood-waters a dark reddish-brown colour similar to blood; they stir up flagellates toxic to fish; prolonged flooding can lead (and has led) to enormous numbers of frogs and biting insects; flies often transmit epidemic diseases of domestic animals ('all the cattle of the Egyptians died'); locusts and sand-storms are common in the Near East. In situations like this it is fairly easy to suggest how God might have worked. The point of the story is not simply to state God's control over the natural world – that is implicit throughout Scripture and is one of the main inferences from the creation accounts in Genesis – but to emphasize his care for his own people and his response to specific prayer.

In most cases, we know no apparent mechanism for particular miracles. For example, it is not clear why the Jordan should be more effective in healing leprosy than 'Abana and Pharpar, the rivers of Damascus' (2 Ki. 5:12), or why Christ used a mud ball to rub the eyes of a blind man (Jn. 9:6). If a modern pathologist had been present at any of the healing miracles, he could in principle have described the changes that took place in the diseased cells of the sufferer as they became healthy, although he would not have been able to say *why* the changes were taking place. Whether we are able to say anything or nothing about the way a miracle was brought about is irrelevant to the purpose of the miracle, and does not affect or detract from the sovereignty of God. A causal explanation is usually on a different level from an explanation which describes divine activity.

It is sometimes asserted that by definition a miracle must happen instantaneously, and in particular that the *fiat* framework of Genesis ('God said, "Let there be . . ." And God saw that it was good') shows that the creation miracles have no time element. This assumption involves a confusion: God is outside time, so it is irrelevant to apply our timescales to him. From the human point of view it is clear that miracles may take some of our time to complete their effect. A particularly clear example of this is Christ's healing of the blind man recorded in Mark 8:23–25, when sight was restored gradually. ('When he had spat on the man's eyes . . . [the man] looked up and said, "I see people; they look like trees walking around" . . . Once more Jesus put his hands on the man's eyes. Then his eyes were opened, his sight was restored, and he saw everything clearly.') Another example is the feeding of the Israelites in the wilderness; manna was provided every day, showing God at work over an extended period.

This brings us back to the connection between God and creation, and the value of seeing God's action and scientific understanding as complementary explanations. The God of the Bible is primarily a creative upholder (Col. 1:17), and only secondarily a divine watchmaker. There is no conflict or rivalry in distinguishing between *why* God created (which is described in the Bible) and the methods or mechanisms used, which it is the business of science to probe. Francis Schaeffer (1973:27) has described how his approach to Genesis 1 changed as he reflected on God's relationship to his creation:

> As a younger Christian, I never thought it right to use the word *creation* for an artist's work. I reserved it for God's initial work alone. But I have come to realise that this was a mistake, because while there is indeed a difference there is a very important parallel. The artist conceives in his thought-world . . . And it is exactly the same with God. God who existed before had a plan, and he created and caused these things to become objective.

In other words, we must distinguish between *why* God created (which is described in the Bible), and the objective *cause*, which is the realm of science. The fact that God created all matter and life, and did not merely shape it, is important. Prior to the action of God 'in the beginning' (Gn. 1:1), there was no other kind of existence than God.

This means that matter is not eternal, and suggests that there is no other power in existence in the universe outside his control. It indicates also, as we have already seen, that God is distinct from his creation, which is not merely an external manifestation of an Absolute (McKay 1982:245). There are several strands of evidence for the doctrine in the Bible. First, there is no mention of any pre-existing material out of which the world was made. Nor do the Scriptures ever represent the world as an emanation from God by a necessity of his nature. Secondly, the descriptions of primary creation rule out any idea of mere formation. 'God said . . .' is the language of Genesis; and in Psalm 33:6 we read, 'By the word of the LORD were the heavens made.' Thirdly, the same doctrine is involved in the absolute dependence of all things on God and in his absolute sovereignty over them. Thus the Israelites led by the Levites addressed God, 'You alone are the LORD. You made the heavens, even the highest heavens, and all their starry host, the earth and all that is on it, the seas and all that is in them. You give life to everything' (Ne. 9:6; see also Col. 1:16–17; Rev. 4:11). Everything other than God is said to owe its existence to his will. Fourthly, the author of Hebrews begins his illustration of the nature and power of faith by referring to creation as the great fundamental truth of all religion (Heb. 11:3). If there is no creation, there is no God; conversely, creation as a divine act is a fact which we know only by revelation. Finally, the doctrine of creation derives from the infinite perfection of God. There can be only one infinite being. If anything exists independently of his will, God is thereby limited. The God of the Bible is an extra-terrestrial God existing outside of and before the world, independent of it, its Creator, preserver and governor. The doctrine of creation is a necessary consequence of theism. Hence the doctrine is presented on the first page of the Bible as the foundation of all subsequent revelations about the nature of God and his relation to the world, and from the beginning one day in seven is appointed as a perpetual commemoration of the fact that God created the heaven and the earth.

God is creator, God is absolute. Where do human beings fit in?

Humankind and the apes

Is man an ape or an angel? My Lord, I am on the side of the Angels.
Benjamin Disraeli in debate with Bishop Wilberforce

We have seen that human beings are closely related to the living apes, indeed that zoologically we *are* apes. We have also seen that it is a major error to regard ourselves as 'nothing but' apes (p. 31). We are not simply apes 'on the way up', but creatures distinguished from all other creatures by being made in God's image (Gn. 1:27; 2:7)

What does this mean? Because Christ was God and took upon himself the form of a human being, it is easy to fall into the trap of assuming that God's image is the same thing as our human form (Wolff 1974; Hoekema 1986). A moment's reflection shows the naïvety of this: the Bible refers to God as having anatomical parts (for instance, eye, arm, even wings: Ps. 36:7, *etc.*), but only when it describes an activity or function; each word presents a picture to help us understand spiritual reality about God and his relationships. The idea of God's image in us being the same as our physical body is as far-fetched as the medieval belief that God resided in the pineal gland (largely on the basis that no function was known for it).

At one time, theologians tended to equate God's image or spirit in human beings with rationality. There is no scriptural support for this, and studies on animals show that they can be as capable of rational thought and learning as we are, albeit to a lesser extent. Indeed, it is difficult to identify absolute differences between the minds of animals and of humans: animals are capable of some degree of aesthetic appreciation and abstract thought; they can have 'nervous breakdowns'; they may 'play' elaborate games; and show considerable community and family care. W. H. Thorpe, one of the most distinguished animal behaviourists, quotes six levels of mental activity described by Hobhouse (1913), of which he could discern four in animals, while the remaining two he regarded as characteristic of humans. Hobhouse called these two 'the correlation of universals' and 'the correlation of governing principles'. They involve a recognition of abstract moral law or, in Thorpe's (1961) words, 'eternal values which are in themselves good'. He justifies this by saying that 'of course we can find in the higher social animals, such as wolves, behaviour which appears altruistic, unselfish, indeed "moral".

Nevertheless I believe at this level we can see a difference between the minds of humans and of present-day animals, and that in Hobhouse's last two categories we have reached a distinction which we can for the time being at least regard as fundamental.'

Modern theological opinion is united in agreeing that the *imago Dei* is non-anatomical; theologians regard God's image as a relational, not a physical, entity. For example, Emil Brunner (1939), commenting on 2 Corinthians 3:18 ('We, who with unveiled faces all reflect the Lord's glory, are being transformed into his likeness . . .'), noted that 'man's meaning and his intrinsic worth do not reside in himself but in the One who stands "over against" him . . . Man's distinctiveness is not based upon the power of his muscles or the acuteness of his sense-organs, but upon the fact that he participates in the life of God, God's thought, and God's will, through the word of God.' C. F. D. Moule (1964) concluded, 'The most satisfying of the many interpretations, both ancient and modern, of the image of God in man is that which sees it as basically responsibility (Ecclesiasticus 17:1–4).' H. D. McDonald (1981) has proposed that 'image should be taken as indicating "sonship" which holds together both the ontological and relational aspects of the image'.

If our humanness is the result of God's work in us, and not a matter of anatomy, physiology and genes, our fossil history is irrelevant (p. 31). However, our more recent history *is* relevant. How realistic is it to believe that there ever was a man called Adam? Genesis describes Adam as a farmer; Pearce (1969) argues that he was cultivating his patch on the slopes of the Turkish plateau as climatic conditions improved following the final retreat of the Pleistocene ice-sheet. This would place him about 10,000 years ago, of the same order as Archbishop Ussher's dating from biblical chronology, of 6,000 years ago.

The evidence for this is what Pearce calls 'a type of cultural zone fossil' in Genesis 2 – 4. First, we are told that 'the LORD God took the man and put him in the garden of Eden to work it and take care of it' (2:15). The particular connection of Adam and Eden with tillage – agriculture – is mentioned three times. In the 'neolithic revolution' our ancestors were able to control their food supply for the first time, which made possible – indeed, required – a settled existence. Secondly, domestication spread rapidly from its believed main origin in the Near East to many parts of temperate Eurasia (11:9). Thirdly, a settled existence led to the possibility of and need for markets and services – in other words, for towns. Among the earliest of these was Catal Huyuk, on the Turkish plateau (4:17). Fourthly, the main diagnostic clue to Adam's culture was that he cultivated crops and bred animals. Early in the record the beginning of metal-working (iron) is noted (4:22). Fifthly, primitive farming is, in modern terminology, labour-intensive. The neolithic revolution permitted and gave rise to the first rapid increase (and hence diversification of occupations) in the human population. We have an emphasis in patriarchal times on massive reproduction (1:28a) and large families. Finally, the climate at the end of the Ice Age was dry and the initial vegetation would have been tundra (2:5), with localized glacial run-offs (2:6), forming oases which probably attracted animals (2:19b). The Garden of Eden is placed (2:10–14) in the region where prehistorians have found the first traces of the neolithic revolution (both archaeological and botanical). The word translated 'Eden' could be the same as the Babylonian 'Edinnu', meaning a plateau or steppes. The land which lies east of the upper reaches of the Tigris was known by the Kassites as Cush, implying that the Gihon was the Araxes and that Eden was in the region assigned to it by Sumerian tradition, at the head water of the great river of Mesopotamia. The cool evenings of 3:8 would be typical of the high plateau.

It is fully consonant with Genesis that God created Adam in the body of a Near Eastern farmer comparatively recently in archaeological terms. If we accept this, the term 'man' as used by the palaeontologist or anthropologist is a much wider term than 'man' as used in the Bible (the existence of pre-Adamic humans conveniently explains such old chestnuts as where Cain got his wife from, and who were the Nephilim, Gn. 6:4); perhaps for clarity we should distinguish *Homo divinus* from *Homo sapiens*. It is certainly worth recording a comment by B. B. Warfield that 'it is to theology as such, a matter of entire indifference how long man has existed on earth'.

What about Eve? Genesis 2:21 tells us that Eve was formed from Adam's side. If God is truly omnipotent, clearly he *could* have made Eve from one of Adam's ribs, but that does not mean that he actually did so. Modern man has the same number of ribs as modern woman. The emphasis of the account is on the similarity of the man and the woman, on their close kinship, and on their possession of an identical essence. Paul states in 1 Corinthians 11:8 that woman was made from (*ek*) man; but this does not require a literal interpretation of Genesis. The old commentator Matthew Henry follows Thomas Aquinas and seems to agree with the spirit of Genesis: God did not make the woman 'out of his head to rule over him, nor out of his feet to be trampled upon by him, but out of his side to be equal with him, under his arm to be protected, and near his heart to be beloved'. More subtly, Augustine regarded the man as the strength of the woman (from him comes the *bone*), while the woman softens the man (in the place of the rib, God closes up the *flesh*). I have no intention of attributing all these meanings to the inspired Author; but he no doubt had several of them in mind, which increases the probability that the writing is figurative.

The fall

The inherent problem about Darwinian humankind evolving upwards from the apes is that we might be expected to be getting better all the time, morally as well as physically. This contrasts with the scriptural position that we are a special creation, inbreathed by God at a specific point in time.

Was there a single historical Adam and a single historical Eve? We should certainly be open to the probability that there are symbolic elements in the first three chapters of Genesis. For example, the serpent which taunted Eve, and the tree of life in the Garden of Eden, reappear in the book of Revelation (*e.g.* 12:9; 22:2ff.), where they appear to be symbols.

But Adam and Eve are different: the Bible seems to intend us to accept their historicity. The biblical genealogies trace the human race back to Adam (Gn. 5:3ff.; 1 Ch. 1:1ff.; Lk. 3:38); Jesus himself taught that at the beginning, the Creator made them male and female and then instituted marriage (Mt. 19:4ff., quoting Gn. 1:27); Paul told the Athenian philosophers that God had made every nation 'from one man' (Acts 17:26); and most notably, Paul's carefully constructed analogy between Adam and Christ depends on the equal historicity of both (Rom. 5:12–19; see also 1 Cor. 15:21, 45). Paul's teaching clearly rests on the fact that 'sin entered the world through one man, and death through sin'. Three points need to be made.

First, the death that came into the world was spiritual (separation from God), not physical death. Adam and Eve 'died' *the day* they disobeyed (Gn. 2:17), but they survived physically (and produced all their family) after their exclusion from God's presence. As John Stott (1994:171) writes, 'Death in Scripture is represented more in legal than in physical terms; not so much as a state of lying motionless but as the grim though just penalty for sin.' When Paul speaks of death entering the world (Rom. 5:12, 18–19), he qualifies it as being visited on all *people*, not on plants and animals.

Secondly, by the time neolithic farming was beginning in the Middle East, *Homo sapiens* had already spread to many parts of the world: there were Indians in America, Aborigines in Australia, and so on. A neolithic Adam and Eve could not be the physical ancestors of the whole human species. But we have already seen that physical relationships are irrelevant where God's human creation is concerned. Spiritual inbreathing and 'spiritual death' are not determined by or spread through Mendelian genes: they depend upon God's distinctive (and divine) methods of transmission. As Kidner (1967:30) has pointed out:

With one possible exception,[4] the unity of mankind 'in Adam' and our common status as sinners through his offence, are expressed in Scripture not in terms of heredity (Is. 43:27) but simply of solidarity. We nowhere find applied to us any argument from physical descent such as that of Hebrews 7:9, 10 (where Levi shares in Abraham's act though being 'still in the loins of his ancestor'). Rather, Adam's sin is shown to have implicated all men because he was the federal head of humanity, somewhat as in Christ's death 'one died for all, therefore all died' (2 Cor. 5:14) . . . After the special creation of the first human pair clinched the fact that there is no natural bridge from animal to man, God may have now conferred his image on Adam's collaterals to bring them into the same realm of being. Adam's 'federal' headship of humanity extended, if that was the case, outwards to his offspring, and his disobedience disinherited both alike.

The Bible's insistence on the spiritual unity of the human race does not necessarily mean a genetical unity, even though this would be the simplest interpretation.

Thirdly, the New Testament passage which most explicitly refers to the fall is Romans 8:18–23. This clearly teaches that the whole creation (including humanity) has been affected by the presence of sin in the world. A closer examination, however, shows that the fall primarily involved disobedient humankind, and only secondarily and consequentially the rest of creation (p. 104).

---

[4] Gn. 3:20, naming Eve as 'mother of all the living'. The concern of the verse, however, is principally to reiterate, in the context of death, the promise of salvation through 'her seed' (Gn. 3:15).

The danger of Romans 8:18–23 is trying to understand it out of its context. It is, in fact, part of the theme of redemption and the Spirit's work which occupies Paul from chapters 5 to 8 of the letter; the passage about the fall and suffering links with Romans 5:3–5, where suffering and hope are associated with the gift of the Spirit. Now the fall resulted in death (Gn. 2:17; Rom. 6:23), that is, separation from God. This had two consequences: the relationship of 'love and cherishing' between Adam and Eve became one of 'desire and domination' (Gn. 3:16; 4:7); and 'tending' in Eden became 'toil' outside (Gn. 3:18; cf. Lv. 26:3ff.; Pr. 2:30–34). Romans 8:20 states that the frustration currently experienced by creation is not innate in it, but was a consequence of 'the will of the one who subjected it'. This was presumably an act of God, because the creation was 'subjected in hope', but the key point is that the frustration arises because of an extrinsic event, and can be dealt with by faith, as Paul points out in Romans 5:2. C. F. D. Moule (1964) paraphrases Romans 8:20: 'For creation was subjected to frustration, not by its own choice but because of Adam's sin which pulled down nature with it, since God had created Adam to be in close connexion with nature.' The teaching of the whole of this central section of Romans is how Christ overcame death (on the cross) and how the consequences of this are dealt with, contrasting life in the flesh with life in the Spirit (6:13). In 8:19 Paul writes about the 'sons of God' who are to be revealed; in the same passage he defines 'sons of God' as 'those who are led by the Spirit of God' (8:14). The next verse (8:20) describes the vanity and frustration which result from a failure to respond to the Spirit. The word translated 'frustration' means literally 'futility' or 'purposelessness'; in other words, the frustration of the non-human world is a consequence of the lack of the care which was ordained for it at creation, when God entrusted its dominion to us. As Kidner says: 'leaderless, the choir of creation can only grind in discord'. The whole of the book of Ecclesiastes is a commentary on this verse.

The message of Romans 8:18–23 is thus one of hope – not looking to the distant future but to the time when the redeemed accept the consequences of their reunion with God, and therefore their responsibility for nature. Paul's argument is that as long as we refuse (or are unable through sin) to play the role God created for us, the world of nature is dislocated and frustrated. Since humankind is God's vicegerent on earth (which is part, at least, of the meaning of being 'in God's image'), he has inevitably failed in his stewardship from the moment he first disobeyed God and dislocated the relationship. Some Christians interpret any facts which they find morally difficult as 'results of the fall' (such as 'nature red in tooth and claw', or the enormous number of human foetuses which spontaneously miscarry). We must be clear that these are no more than guesses; we are almost completely ignorant about the moral state of affairs before the fall (although we know that there were landslides and extensive floods on earth before there is any evidence of human life, and that many dinosaurs suffered from arthritis). It is highly dubious exegesis to argue from such apocalyptic passages as Isaiah 11:6–9 ('The wolf will live with the lamb . . .') that particular ecological conditions were God's primary purpose. Hugh Ross (1994:63) comments:

> Considering how creatures convert chemical energy into kinetic energy, we can say that carnivorous activity results from the laws of thermodynamics, not from sin. Large, active, agile land animals must spend virtually all their waking hours grazing, drinking or digesting or they must consume meat . . . We tend to anthropomorphize and thus distort the sufferings of animals. But even plants suffer when they are eaten . . .

Conclusions

The begetter of much modern 'creationism'[5] is the Adventist George McCready Price (1870–1963) (Numbers 1992). His clarion call was, 'No Adam, no fall; no fall, no atonement; no atonement, no Saviour.' His message was that belief in Christianity is completely incompatible with belief in evolution. He was wrong. There are three possible views about human origins: as 'nothing but' a highly evolved ape; as 'nothing but' a special creation of God made complete in every respect; or as an ape inbreathed by God's Spirit, with an evolutionary history but with a unique relationship with the Creator. Only the last can incorporate both a sensible understanding of Scripture and the findings of science. But even more important, only the last does justice to the God of the Bible, who is both Creator and Sustainer.

The tragedy of the 'creationist' position and the danger of the debate stirred by 'creationists' is that it hides the glorious irony of the Darwinian revolution: Darwin brought God back into his world from his exclusion

[5] All Christians who profess to 'believe in God . . . maker of heaven and earth' are properly called creationists. I use inverted commas to emphasize that 'creationist' is now being used (and claimed) in a very restricted sense.

'out there' by theologians of the eighteenth and nineteenth centuries. Nineteenth-century deism was inadequate; only when God is seen to be both immanent and transcendent (which is what the Bible teaches, *e.g.* Eph. 4:6) will Christianity become relevant once more. Science can speak only of a mechanistic causality, while the Bible speaks of a purposive one; the intellectual climate of modern humankind makes necessary, both scientifically and theologically, a God who is active in his world.

It is worth stressing this. To many people, Christianity is not so much wrong as unnecessary. There is no virtue and no hope in believing in a First Cause who is impotent in the world he created. But the evolutionary controversy has forced us to recognize that any religion worth serious consideration must be one whose God is in constant control of everyday events. Our God is too often too small; he is one who has redeemed us and who is working his purposes out, but one whom we do not like to recognize in the events of everyday living. Consequently we profess a desiccated and gutless Christianity utterly divorced from that of the New Testament church, as well as from that of Luther, Cranmer, Simeon, Wesley, Booth, Moody and Temple. Let us affirm that God has worked and is working through normal, scientifically analysable events (as well as through the miraculous supernatural); he is in control of our body as well as our soul; we need fear no secular discoveries because true faith is independent of although complementary to them. The Royal Society was founded by men who wanted to know how God was working in the world. May that be our attitude as well!

This is, of course, where the purpose of living, identified by George Porter as our great need, comes in (p. 29). Life is not a mere lottery or a predetermined biological path; it is an adventure filled with choices, and a pilgrimage planned by the one who has gone before (Heb. 7:18–19). Science describes order and disorder; it cannot explain evil. In contrast, Christianity answers evil and helps us find the niche prepared for us.

This may be a secular or a religious search. Thor Heyerdahl, who attained fame with his *Kon-Tiki* and *Ra* voyages, planned as a young man to escape the constraints and artificiality of modern living. With his wife, he 'dropped out' and went to live on an 'unspoilt' tropical island with only 'unspoilt' natives for company. After a year he returned to his native Norway and wrote:

There is no Paradise to be found on earth today. There are people living in great cities who are far happier than the majority of those in the South Seas.

Happiness comes from within, we realize that now . . . It is in his mind and way of life that man may find his Paradise – the ability to perceive the true values of life, which are far removed from property and riches, or from power and renown (Jacoby 1968:69).

But not all experiences are negative. Ernest Shackleton, after an 800-mile crossing of the Antarctic Ocean in an open boat, landed on the barren south shore of South Georgia. He and his companions had to cross the unexplored high interior of the island to reach human settlement. He later described this:

I know that during that long and racking march of thirty-six hours over the unnamed mountains and glaciers of South Georgia it seemed to me often that we were four, not three. I said nothing to my companions on the point, but afterwards Worsley said to me, 'Boss, I had a curious feeling on the march that there was another person with us.' Crean confessed to the same idea.

Frank Smyth had a not dissimilar experience at over 28,000 ft on Mount Everest: 'All the time I was climbing alone I had the strong feeling that I was accompanied by a second person. This feeling was so strong that it eliminated all loneliness that I might otherwise have felt.' He even divided his mint-cake, and 'it was almost a shock to find no-one to give it to'.

It is easy to be cynical or clinical about such stories, but if God is really with us it would not be surprising if he sometimes became disconcertingly vivid, although it would be dangerous to expect him to appear to order, or to make our faith depend on specific senses. The general rule is, surely, that God in Christ is *always* with us; after all, 'in him all things hold together' (Col. 1:17). We must remain open to the possibility that God could break into our experience at any point, and not merely when we expect him. John Polkinghorne (1983:54) has written:

In an earlier age, miracles would have been one of the strongest weapons in the armoury of apologetic. A man who did such things must at the very least have the power of God with him. Jesus himself is represented as using this argument when he said, 'If it is by the finger of God that I cast out demons, then the kingdom of God has come upon you' (Lk. 11:20 [RSV]). For us today, by one of the twists that make up intellectual history, miracles are rather an embarrassment. We are so impressed by the regularity of the world that any story which is full of strange happenings acquires an air of fairytale and invention.[6]

At this point one is tempted to agree with the author of Ecclesiastes, that 'of making many books there is no end, and much study wearies the body . . . Here is the conclusion of the matter: Fear God and keep his commandments, for this is the whole duty of man' (Ec. 12:12–13). But this could be regarded as somewhat anti-rational, and it is my firm contention that we must use our minds as well as our bodies in the Lord's service. So I conclude this chapter with the research scientists' text, carved (in Latin) on the gates of the Cavendish Physics Laboratory of the University of Cambridge:

> Great are the works of the LORD;
> they are pondered by all who delight in them.
>
> (Ps. 111:2)

[6] It is worth noting that as C. S. Lewis (1947:106) has pointed out, David Hume's proof that miracles do not occur is not as strong as it is often claimed to be. We must agree with Hume that if there is absolute "uniform experience" against miracles, if in other words they have never happened, why then they never have. Unfortunately we know the experience against them to be uniform only if we know that all the reports of them are false. And we know the reports to be false only if we know already that miracles have never occurred. In fact, we are arguing in a circle.'

4

GENES AND GENESIS

One of the commonest assumptions about human biology is that we are imprisoned by our genes: that the blueprint laid down when our father's sperm fertilized our mother's ovum determines not only our sex and size and liability to disease, but also our desires, abilities and moral quirks. This is a gross over-exaggeration, owing more to Aldous Huxley and *Brave New World* (first published in 1932) than to the science of genetics, but it is very widespread. Although it is true that if two particular gametes (sperm and egg) had not fused nine months before I was born, I would not be here, it does not follow that the 'genetic code' of the 20,000 or so genes on the forty-six chromosomes of my body gives a complete or even adequate specification of me. There is both scientific and moral evidence for the falsity of this assumption.

Genetics and epigenetics

The DNA of the chromosomes is 'translated' into chains of amino acids (polypeptide chains), which in turn form proteins and enzymes. But the production of polypeptide chains is not an automatic process that goes on throughout life. Genes are subject to precise control or regulation, with many (indeed, most) being switched off most of the time. The genes in every cell in the body are affected by the history and environment of that cell, and the bulk of the chromosome set which is replicated and found in the nucleus of most body cells is non-functional. Cells in which this control process breaks down are liable (if they survive) to be cancer-producing.

The development and functioning of a whole organism are even more complicated. Some of the proteins that are primary gene products are recognizable in a normal body; they turn up as enzymes controlling vital processes or antigens affecting particular immunological reactions. But the primary products of most genes interact in the body to form secondary compounds, which are the main building-blocks for growth and maintenance, hormones and so on. These interactions are highly complex and specific; in no way can the human body be regarded as the automatic consequence of a set of random chemical specifications. Although virtually all our characters can be regarded as affected by genes, their inheritance and control should be described as *epigenetic* rather than genetic; in other words, it is the result of processes acting subsequently to the primary action of the genes themselves.

The primary gene products are the direct consequence of a rather simple chemical process that has been worked out in the revolution of molecular biology begun in 1955 with the elucidation of the structure of DNA by James Watson and Francis Crick. At this level, inherited characters can be said to be determined by the genes carried by an individual. Once we leave the primary gene product level, however, the occurrence, speed and direction of the chemical processes in the body are affected to varying extents by environmental influences. This is of considerable importance in clinical medicine, because inherited defects in metabolism can often be corrected once they have been identified. For example, diabetes can be treated with insulin, haemophilia with anti-haemophilic globulin, and phenylketonuria and galactosaemia by with-holding from the diet phenylalanine and galactose respectively. One of the aims of the Human Genome Project is to advance these possibilities (Bryant 1992). It is not true that genetic disease cannot be treated, as used to be believed.

The interaction of genes and environment applies throughout normal development. Prenatal growth is slowed if the mother smokes, and maternal drinking may reduce the intelligence and size of a baby at birth (foetal alcohol syndrome). Childhood growth can be affected by nutrition. IQ is higher in first children, and in small families than in larger ones.

It is difficult to work out the details of interactions between genes and environment in humans, where experimental breeding and environ-mental control cannot be carried out. Comparison of the behaviour and achievements of identical and non-identical twins, and of adopted and natural children, can go some way to helping us understand these processes, but unchallenged conclusions are very few, as the recurring debates on the inheritance of intelligence show. Criminality and sexual deviation have often been attributed either to family or to inherited influences, but the grounds for distinguishing between these tend to be equivocal. Notwithstanding, there can be no doubt at all that we are affected radically by our environments as well as by our genes.

The genetic control of behaviour has been much discussed in recent years. For my purpose, all that it is necessary to note is that few behavioural traits are irrevocably determined by genes; virtually all human behaviour (and associated characters, like intelligence) can be unintentionally or consciously influenced by the environment. Although it is true that we can speak of behaviour as being inherited, it is equally true and perhaps more helpful to recognize that there is no one gene for any specific behaviour.

This is well shown by identical twins (that is, genetically identical individuals), who are often strikingly alike in both behaviour and physical traits even when reared apart, but there are plenty of examples where identical twin pairs show marked and significant differences for some characters. Genes cannot express themselves in a vacuum; even in cases where our genes predispose us towards certain characters (as a shallow hip-joint to congenital hip dislocation, or an extra Y chromosome to mindless aggression), there is no automatic association between a gene and the physical or behavioural trait that finally emerges.

There is also no simple relationship between a fertilized egg and survival to adult life. For every 100 eggs subject to normal internal fertilization, 85 will be fertilized if intercourse is frequent, 69 are implanted, 42 are alive a week later, 37 at the sixth week of gestation, and 31 at birth. Between a third and a half of the foetuses that abort spontaneously in the first few weeks of pregnancy (that is, with no human intervention) have an abnormal chromosomal complement; 97% of foetuses with a single sex chromosome (Turner's syndrome) and 65–70% of those with Down's syndrome (mongolism) have miscarried by the eighteenth week. It seems likely that a large proportion of embryos with anomalies of the central nervous system (anencephaly, spina bifida and so on) are spontaneously aborted, and so survival to birth is not the norm; it occurs in only a minority of conceptuses, and many of those eliminated are recognizably abnormal in their genetic complement.

When we consider together interactions between different genes, interactions between genes and the environment, and foetal death, it is obvious that we are determined by our genes only in a very loose sense. Some of the differences between us are the result of different genetic complements, but these differences can be magnified or diminished by family, social, educational, cultural or other environmental influences. Even people whose hereditary make-up irrevocably fixes some traits – such as those with Down's syndrome – nevertheless show a wide range of behavioural responses (in the case of a Down's individual, from gross mental defect to near normality).

Clearly there is a sense in which we must be regarded as the sum of the genes we acquire at conception, but in another sense we are considerably more than that sum. Just as the wetness of water cannot be predicted from the atomic properties of its constituent hydrogen and oxygen, so human beings cannot adequately be described by their genes, even if we knew the details of all the DNA of an individual.

Genes and morals

Moralists traditionally argue that ethical decisions cannot be controlled by genes. One reason for this is that positive virtues might be expected to hinder their possessors in the struggle for existence. Charles Darwin himself spelt out the problem in *The Descent of Man* (1871):

> It is extremely doubtful whether the offspring of the more sympathetic and benevolent parents, or of those who were the most faithful to their comrades, would be reared in greater numbers than the children of selfish and treacherous parents belonging to the same tribe. He who was ready to sacrifice his life, as many a savage has been, rather than betray his comrades, would often leave no offspring to inherit his noble nature. The bravest men, who were always willing to come to the front in war, and who freely risked their lives for others, would on average perish in larger numbers than other men. Therefore it hardly seems probable that the number of men gifted with such virtues, or the standard of their excellence, could be increased through natural selection, that is, by the survival of the fittest.

Half a century later, J B. S. Haldane (1932) qualified this, pointing out that if the unselfishness (even to the point of self-sacrifice) of an individual had an inherited basis, and if it helped near relatives, then 'altruistic genes' could be selected in families; there could be situations where co-operation (that is, unselfishness) is an advantage to a group of relatives. Haldane's argument was formalized in 1964 by W. D. Hamilton as the concept of 'inclusive fitness' or (as it has since become known) 'kin selection'.

The 1950s and 1960s saw much interest in biology and behaviour, shown in the writings of Konrad Lorenz, Niko Tinbergen, Vero Wynne-Edwards, Robert Ardrey and Desmond Morris, later expressed in such television series as David Attenborough's *Life on Earth* (1979). Socio-biology entered common language with the publication of a book called *Sociobiology: The New Synthesis* by Edward Wilson (1975), a distinguished entomologist who had spent many years studying social insects (such as ants, termites and bees). In his book, Wilson ranged widely through the animal kingdom, concluding with a chapter entitled 'Man: From Sociobiology to Sociology', in which he applied conclusions about genes and behaviour from (mainly) invertebrates to human beings. He later expanded this chapter into a book called *On Human Nature* (1978). In this, Wilson expounded sociobiology as providing a biological under-pinning for all the human sciences: 'Biology is the key to human nature, and social scientists cannot afford to ignore its rapidly tightening principles.' Wilson has been attacked by both sociologists and socialists, who see his ideas as contrary to their dreams of improving society by manipulating the environment. We are not concerned with these here; they are driven more by political conceptions and correctness than by science. What we are concerned with is the attempt to portray sociobiology as the complete explanation of altruism. The Australian philosopher Peter Singer (1981:49) has written:

> Sociobiology . . . enables us to see ethics as a mode of human reasoning which develops in a group context . . . so ethics loses its air of mystery. Its principles are not laws written up in Heaven. Nor are they absolute truths about the universe, known by intuition. The principles of ethics come from our own nature as social reasoning beings.

It must be emphasized that this statement has no support from science. Our behaviour is affected by our genes but is certainly not controlled by it. The argument is too often heard that a person cannot be held responsible for some action because of his inherited disposition – towards alcohol, academic work, homosexual acts or even traits such as punctuality or tidiness. When a high proportion of tall men committed to institutions for the criminal insane on account of their aggressiveness were found to have an extra Y chromosome (that is, to be XYY), their disability was hailed as proving the inheritance of original sin – until other XYY men were found living perfectly normal lives in the community.

I have already argued that there is no such thing as a behavioural gene; every behaviour is the result of interactions between inherited and environmental factors (p. 61). Important among these environmental factors are the constraints regulating society; overriding them are the interactions that make us 'body-souls'.

Paul was well aware of the tensions producing immorality: 'What I do is not the good I want to do; no, the evil I do not want to do – this I keep on doing' (Rom. 7:19). Notwithstanding, he distinguished explicitly between temptation and sin (1 Cor. 10:13; 2 Tim. 3:1ff.); an alternative way of describing much temptation is as inherited predisposition. No behaviour is inevitable.

Let us be quite clear about moral weakness: different people have different natures and therefore different problems, and some of these may need medical correction (for instance, depression or schizophrenia). But the ultimate sanction is God's judgment, and the essential therapy must include God's grace (Phil. 4:13).

Genes, character and talents

Genetic orientation reduces neither moral responsibility or culpability, but we all know that genes influence our talents and characters. This was first formalized by Francis Galton (1822–1911), Charles Darwin's cousin. Galton took from contemporary encyclopedias details about leading jurists, statesmen, military commanders, scientists, poets, painters and musicians. He found that a disproportionately high proportion of them were blood relatives, and concluded that 'families of reputation' were much more likely to produce offspring of ability than ordinary families. He documented this in his *Hereditary Genius* (1869). It convinced him that it would be 'quite practicable to produce a highly gifted race of men by judicious marriages during several consecutive generations'. He believed that talent was rarely damaged by social disadvantages, as witness the men of achievement who came from humble families. Notwithstanding, removal of disadvantage does not produce talent by itself. He wrote: 'Culture is far more widely spread in America than with us [in Britain], and the education of their middle and lower classes far more advanced; but for all that, America most certainly does not beat us in first-class works of literature, philosophy or art.'

Such considerations led Galton to propose the importance of 'eugenics', the encouragement of breeding for good traits and selecting against deleterious ones. The sorry history of eugenics, particularly when linked to Herbert Spencer's 'social Darwinism' and the perversions of a pantheon of racialists, does not concern us here, although it is worth noting, in passing, the dangers of building too much upon incomplete axioms (there is no doubt that there are more differences between individuals than between races).[1] From the present perspective, the problem is that inherited characteristics and human reproduction are combined and confused in popular understanding (Gould 1981; Kevles 1985). The unravelling of the genetic code and the possibilities of genetic manipulation have put genetics (and geneticists) near the top of the modern demonology.

Reproductive technology

In fact the extraordinary achievements of molecular genetics are only just beginning to make an impact on the human species. Much more important so far have been developments in reproductive technology. Although the details of sexual reproduction were not worked out until the 1870s (traditionally, the man was the one who provided the seed, the woman the field in which it was sown and nurtured), couples have attempted to influence the results of their coupling from the earliest times. Hippocrates, for example, believed that males developed more commonly on the right side of the uterus and females on the left. This led to the assumption that sperm from the right testis were likely to produce males, and to the practice of ligating (or even removing) the left testis if a son was desired. Rabbi Isaac (in the *Talmud*, third century AD) taught

---

[1] The Bible nowhere teaches that we are all the same; rather, its whole emphasis is on distinctions, although these are of achievement and aptitude rather than status (Mt. 25:14–30; Mk. 4:8; 1 Cor. 12:27–30; Eph. 4:11; *etc.*). It should not be surprising that human populations are composed of men and women with varied talents. Modern society complicates this heterogeneity by rewarding some talents more than others (numeracy more than physical strength, beauty more than longevity, and so on), but we ought not to allow ourselves to graft ideas of moral worth on to the underlying diversity of human populations. Every society needs refuse collectors as much as chess-players, shopkeepers as much as poets, lawyers as much as car mechanics.

that a boy was the likely result if the woman had an orgasm before the man. More recent attempts to affect the sex of the desired child include vaginal douching, dietary additives and various chemical and physical attempts to separate X from Y sperm (that is, female-determining from male-determining). Other reproductive lore is more soundly based. For example, the *Talmud* exempts a male Jewish child from circumcision if his mother has any relatives who are 'bleeders' (haemophiliacs); this does not apply to relatives of the father. In other words, the Jews have had a working knowledge of sex-linked inheritance for many centuries.

The earliest recorded case of artificial insemination was in 1790, when an Aberdeen doctor inseminated a London woman with her husband's semen because the husband was unable to have normal intercourse, and a child resulted. The first known successful insemination by donor was in Philadelphia in 1884. With around one couple in ten sterile, DI (donor insemination, formerly referred to as AID, artificial insemination by donor, but whose name was changed to avoid confusion with Aids) has become increasingly common during the present century, particularly since techniques for freezing sperm became available. It was condemned in 1948 by a Commission set up by the Archbishop of Canterbury on the ground that it made a personal act into a 'transaction', and then in 1949 by Pope Pius XII because it involved masturbation and also because it introduced a split between procreation and personhood. (This was reaffirmed in 1968 by Pope Paul VI in *Humanae Vitae* and in 1993 by John Paul II in *Veritatis Splendor*). Prior to this, the Lambeth Conference of Anglican bishops had accepted in 1930 that procreation can be separated from the other goods of marriage (emotional or relational, and faithfulness or moral discipline) when they agreed the legitimacy of artificial contraception, although their reasons were pragmatic (economic depression, abhorrence of abortion as a means of contraception, and the changed role of women in society) rather than doctrinal.

The situation became suddenly more acute, however, in 1978, when Louise Brown was born in a hospital in the north of England, to a lawfully married couple after an entirely normal pregnancy. But conception had taken place outside the mother's body by *in vitro* fertilization (IVF); in common parlance, Louise Brown was a 'test-tube baby'. Reproductive scientists had been warning for years that IVF was likely to happen, but for most people it was no more than science fiction. Notwithstanding, Louise Brown's birth was a fact and was entirely legal.

Under English law no offence had been committed by the scientists and doctors who treated her parents.

IVF and parallel technologies are now practised in many countries of the world, and many legislatures have struggled to regulate them in an acceptable and reasonable way. I can speak with authority only about the situation in Britain, but this is of more than local interest because the British legislation is the first comprehensive law to be enacted, following an extended period of debate which involved general arguments as well as special pleading.

Once the dust had settled on the immediate aftermath of Louise Brown's birth, the British Government set up in 1982 a Committee of Inquiry chaired by a moral philosopher, Mary Warnock, 'to consider recent and potential developments in medicine and science related to human fertilization and embryology; to consider what policies and safeguards should be applied, including consideration of the social, ethical and legal implications of these developments; and to make recommendations.'

At its first meeting, the Committee decided that its remit included sex selection and artificial insemination, but not abortion or contraception. It invited views on its task, and was deluged with evidence from a wide range of bodies, professional and lay, religious and secular. It would be good to think that Christians were helpful to it, but, as Bob Edwards (the scientist responsible for Louise Brown's conception) commented of his own search for moral guidelines:

> We have looked for inspiration to philosophers, theologians, lawyers, for their wisdom gained over centuries of debate about ethics, about human standards in relation to the implications of new work. This search for advice, for leadership, for clarity from the traditional purveyors of moral standards, usually ends in confusion. There is confusion between the great religions of the world . . . It is the same with philosophers . . . Nor do the lawyers give us any help (Edwards 1983).

The philosophers Peter Singer and Deane Wells (1983) are more pungent: 'The difficulty is that those upon whom God could most reasonably be expected to have vouchsafed revelation do not all seem to be in possession of the same information.'

The Warnock Committee produced its Report in 1984 and, after further consultation and debate both within and without the UK

Parliament, a Human Fertilization and Embryology Act was passed in 1990. I comment below on the outworkings of the Act, but first I want to lay out the theological issues. I do this from a close involvement in the debates; I chaired a Working Party for the General Synod of the Church of England to advise the Church on 'Warnock matters'. Our Report, *Personal Origins*, was published in 1985 by the Church Information Office and subsequently accepted by the General Synod.

There were three major areas of concern: first, the status of the fertilized egg or early embryo, and the protection it should be given; secondly, the nature of the marriage bond, and the effect on it of the introduction of a third (or even fourth) party as happens in DI, ovum donation, and so on; and thirdly the nature and extent of divine providence and human responsibility.

Underlying all three points (although directly relevant to the first) is our understanding of the nature of life, and particularly of the relation of God to such life. What we had to do was develop a case-history based on the general features of the relationship between God and his creation (p. 68). Particularly germane would be our understanding of 'humanness'; this, as we have already seen, is not equivalent to biological life, albeit intimately related (p. 48). In examining these questions, it is helpful to consider them under the traditional three divisions of tradition, reason (which for the present purpose we can effectively equate with science) and Scripture.

Tradition

There is a general assumption that the long-standing tradition of Christians is that life begins at conception. This tends to be treated as a self-evident affirmation. In fact it became common only as an implication of a papal Bull of 1854 on the immaculate conception of the Blessed Virgin Mary (Dunstan 1984). Prior to this time, the dominant Christian tradition (as set out in both canon law and in English common law, which prescribed the penalties for carrying out an abortion) was that killing a foetus in the first two or three months of gestation was not punishable as homicide, although still regarded as a serious misdemeanour and not approved by the church.

The earlier tradition was based on Aristotelian embryology as interpreted by the early Christian fathers (notably Augustine) and supported by Bible exposition. The Greeks regarded the earliest embryonic stages as plant-like, needing and drawing nourishment like any other plant; the embryo then became an animal creature, sensitive and responsive like other animals; and finally a creature having human features like themselves. They saw the outward form as the projection of inward animating principles (Greek *psychē*, Latin *anima*, soul); animating the plant was a vegetative soul, and animating the human form was a rational soul. Until the embryo began to have human form it lacked human animation; in the western moral and legal traditions *formatus* and *animatus* became criteria for the recognition of the right of a being to be protected.

This interpretation accorded with the understanding of Exodus 21:22–23, which is the only reference to abortion in the Bible. These verses clearly affirm a worth for foetal life, but neither their application nor indeed their translation (Dunstan 1984) is straightforward. The Septuagint says that life is to be given for life if a 'formed' embryo is killed. Both Jerome and Augustine argued that the act was not to be taken to be homicide if the foetus was 'unformed', 'for there cannot yet be said to be a live soul in a body which lacks sensation when it is not formed in the flesh and so not yet endowed with sense' (Augustine on the Latin text of Ex. 21:22). While both Jerome and Augustine remained agnostic about the point at which the soul entered the body, they were not prepared to affirm with confidence that this had taken place while the foetus was 'unformed'.

The modern use of these verses is not helped by versions which translate the Hebrew (which speaks, literally, of 'departing fruit') as miscarriage (RSV, NEB) or the even more emotive 'gives birth prematurely' (NIV). Notwithstanding modern translations, for almost 1,500 years the dominant Christian tradition gave full protection only to a 'formed' embryo. In practice, the time of transition from unformed to formed was taken as 'quickening', when a mother begins to feel her·foetus moving. Thomas Aquinas wrote of Exodus 21:22–23, 'If death should result either for the woman or for the animated foetus (*puerperii animati*), he who strikes cannot escape the crime of homicide . . . The conception of a male is not completed until about the fortieth day, as Aristotle says; that of a female until about the ninetieth day.' Scriptural support for the idea that the soul enters a male foetus at forty days and a female at ninety (derived from the time of ritual cleansing after childbirth as laid down in Lv. 12:1–5) was claimed in papal edicts in the thirteenth and sixteenth centuries.

Embryologists do not now recognize a major distinction between a formed and an unformed foetus, and many modern expositors assume therefore that the traditional understanding is wrong. This is a misunderstanding of embryological development, which involves a series of threshold events. If (as there are good reasons to believe) the maturing nervous system goes through a sequence of stages in which qualitatively new modes of co-operative activity arise, some of which are known in later life to be essential for the maintenance of conscious personal agency, then even complete continuity of biological development would not rule out the possibility of a 'decisive moment', or at least a decisive stage, before which there is 'nobody there', but after which there is 'someone' who is a 'he' or a 'she' as a personal cognitive agent, however limited in capacities. If, on the other hand, we believe that there is no real step in a continuous process and therefore there is no distinction between the beginning and end of the process, we may be in danger of falling into 'thin edge of wedgery' (MacKay 1984; Williams 1985). However, we have only to think of the process by which a hairless chin becomes bearded, or an increasingly rich mixture of gas and air becomes a flame, or – most relevantly to our purpose – a slowly deteriorating human organism becomes a dead body, to see the fallacy of this second form of argument. In all these cases what we have at one end of the process is qualitatively different from what we have at the other. No amount of evidence of continuity at the physical level could justify us in denying or blurring the distinction between the two ends, however difficult it may be to identify the decisive moment at which one turns into the other.

Despite modern glosses, it is worth emphasizing that the longest-lasting Christian tradition has been that early foetuses do not warrant the same degree of protection as later ones, and that this distinction was based firmly on a respect for and application of Scripture. It is also worth noting that the official (and current) Roman Catholic Declaration on Abortion (1974) is explicitly agnostic about the status of the earliest embryos: 'This declaration deliberately leaves aside at what moment in time the spiritual soul is infused. On this matter tradition is not unanimous and writers differ. Some assert it happens at the first instance of life, while others consider that it does not happen before the seed has taken up its position.'

Another strand of tradition maintains that the key to understanding humanity is not biology but personhood. Unfortunately this does not help us to determine the beginning of life, because it is still necessary to determine the beginning of personhood. We have already noted the irrelevance of our genes to the image of God in us. The protagonists of the view that life begins at conception must base their case on the importance of the zygote formed by fusion of gametes, but at the same time they are forced to play down any physical attributes of the conceptus, lest they be taken as identifying the person who will develop with particular traits. For example, O'Donovan (1984:50), while acknowledging that the expression 'personhood' is non-biblical, has argued for its importance as defining something which is disclosed rather than conferred, and which we recognize only because of a prior moral commitment. In contrast, Mahoney (1984:54–55) urges that

> . . . the idea of person (as existing from the fertilizaton of the ovum) has moved so far from ordinary usage and become so attenuated and blurred, so distanced from ordinary understanding as to be now altogether meaningless, and indeed misleading . . . The debate is not clarified by introducing the idea of potential, since its use on both sides simply reflects and extends (opposing) fundamental positions. Those who would argue that to describe the conceptus as only potentially a human person is to ignore the fact that even the child at birth is still only potentially a human person are using the term 'potential' to mean the capacity to become more of a person, or more fully a person, in terms of characteristically personal activities. While on the other hand, those who claim that this description of a potential human person applies exclusively to the embryo or foetus at an early stage are using the term 'potential' to mean that it is not yet in any real sense a person at all. Personhood is perhaps the most ambiguous term in the whole discussion.

Reason

The two essential characteristics of biological life are replication and mutation. If there were no mutation, there would be no variation; we would all be identical. In the Bible, life has the implication of 'activity' or 'necessities for maintenance'. This does not fit easily with other common ways in which we use the word. These include the physiological, which is continuous through all generations, presumably from a unique beginning; the genetical, where uniqueness is established at gamete formation in the parents of a child, since fertilization is merely the adding together of two unique entities; the embryological, which is stimulated and can therefore be regarded as initiated by fertilization; and the spiritual, which implies the ability of fellowship or communication with God.

To the Bible writers (and for many centuries after them), 'life' was a great mystery. *Cogito ergo sum* was as near as secular thought could get to

KING ALFRED'S COLLEGE
LIBRARY

describing it. We can now describe physical life in great detail (Ford 1988). Some laboratory experiments have come close to making 'new' life. We know a considerable amount about the molecular biology of human reproduction. At that level life is continuous: gametogenesis, fertilization, embryogenesis, birth, growth, reproduction and fertilization can be divided into recognizable periods, but the divisions are arbitrary. Furthermore, the gametes are genetically just as unique as the fertilized ovum; the embryo is unable to live independently of its mother for at least four or five months after fertilization (and nowadays that stage is more dependent on technology than on biology); it is worth noting that a cancer is a genetically unique event, and a hydatidiform mole is a unique product of the fusion of sperm and ovum. Neither uniqueness nor independent existence can be used as a measure of moral worth.

Moreover, there is no certainty of continuity from conception to birth or beyond. We have already noted that around two thirds of conceptuses are lost, many before implantation and the majority with chromosomal defects (p. 61). The loss of so many fertilized ova does not prove anything, but it makes the assumption that life (in its fullest sense) begins at conception rather odd.

But perhaps the biggest problem from science for the protagonists of the view that life begins at conception is the occurrence of twinning by splitting of an early embryo. This may happen at any time up to ten days or so after fertilization, and leads to identical twins who are usually entirely normal. No-one doubts that such twins are normal human beings in God's sight, yet if their humanness were established at conception, they would have (in crude language) only half a soul each.[2] Even worse perhaps is the rare fusion of binovular twins formed from two sperm and two ova. Such an individual has four 'parents', yet again can be entirely normal.

Reason does not prove anything certain about 'humanness', but it raises problems about naïvely assuming that life begins at conception.

Scripture

There are many references in the Bible to life before birth. The Psalms

---

[2] We do not *have* souls; we *are* souls. The notion of the soul as an entity is derived from Plato and Aristotle rather than the Bible. But it is an idea which has infected Christian thinking down the centuries. For a scriptural discussion of human nature see Myers & Jeeves (1987).

often refer to God's care and protection in the womb (notably Ps. 139:13–16; see also Ps. 119:73; Jb. 10:8; 31:15). Both Isaiah and Jeremiah refer to being called before birth (Is. 49:1, 5; Je. 1:5), indeed, Jeremiah's call came *before* he was 'formed . . . in the womb'. But in an even more remarkable way, our own choosing as Christians was 'before the creation of the world' (Eph. 1:4; *cf.* 2 Tim. 1:9.) Luke uses the same Greek word (*brephos*) to describe the unborn John the Baptist, the newborn Jesus, and the children brought to Jesus for blessing (Lk. 1:41, 44; 2:12, 16; 18:15).

Since God's calling can precede intra-uterine life, there cannot be a complete identity between physical and spiritual life. The argument that spiritual life is coincident with physical origins, because Christ was God incarnate from the moment when the Holy Spirit came upon Mary (Lk. 1:35), and therefore that all spiritual life begins at conception, demands extrapolating from our Lord's divinity in a way which is improper for a unique event; it was theologically necessary for Christ's parentage to be different from ours if he was to be truly God as well as wholly human (Berry 1996). It can be countered by the statement of the Preacher that 'you do not know how the spirit comes to the bones in the womb of a woman with child' (Ec. 11:5, RSV).

The verses that involve an individual's looking back to acknowledge God's care over him or her at all stages of life (most often quoted in the context is 'You [God] knit me together in my mother's womb', Ps. 139:13) can apply only to the retrospect of a rational being.

It is not legitimate to argue that since God was involved with *me* from conception, therefore he is 'in' all conceptuses. Indeed, to do so is comparable to the mistake of arguing from his trustworthiness in arranging our destiny to the theological necessity of a geocentric universe; it puts us back with the Galileo debate again. Psalm 139 emphatically confirms the divine sovereignty over and through every event in and through which actual living *persons* have gained their embodiment. Once a *person* exists, one must reckon with his or her whole life history as a linked sequence of divinely guided and appointed processes and events. But Psalm 139 says nothing whatsoever about those who are not 'persons'. We have no biblical authority for saying that there was a 'person' present in every spontaneously aborted fertilized ovum, despite all its marvellous complexities and potentialities. If we are honest, we need to be agnostic about the relationship between God and early embryos. He *may* be involved with and overseeing every fertilized egg, but the balance of tradition, reason and Scripture is that there is no direct evidence for it, and the balance of probability is against it.

We have already discussed the effect of the fall on humans (p. 51), but it is pertinent to repeat that while the fall had tangible effects, there is no general agreement regarding what they were. It is wrong, however, to claim that humans must have undergone genetical change when they 'fell'. This becomes immediately apparent if we consider the implication of any genetical change produced by Adam's disobedience: it could in principle be reversed by genetical engineering techniques. This possibility is not dependent upon the limitations of available technology or the morality of attempting such an interference. The point is that a genetical fall could be dealt with biochemically, with no need for Christ's redeeming work. It must necessarily be concluded that the fall was not a genetical event. This supports the idea that genes are, as it were, morally neutral;[3] and goes against (although it does not contradict) the likelihood that fertilization (which is simply a fusion of paternally and maternally derived genes) is a morally crucial event.

The nature of marriage and the family

The next consideration from Scripture is the nature of marriage. God ordained marriage in the first place for companionship (Gn. 2:18, 24; Mt. 19:5). There is a strong historical tradition that the relational and procreational 'goods' of marriage can be separated only improperly (p. 66); Paul's emphasis on the 'one flesh' of marriage is part of this tradition (1 Cor. 6:16; Eph. 5:31). The teaching about 'one flesh', however, is not intrinsically about reproduction, but about the complementarity of male and female. The biblical usage of 'flesh' refers to much more than our

---

[3] It is not accurate to speak of genes as being intrinsically 'bad' or 'deleterious', but only to recognize that a characteristic may be harmful in a particular environment. In the sense that genes are created entities, they are 'good', but only in the same way that buttercups or beetles (say) are good. Short-sightedness is a problem to a hunter, but can be repaired by spectacles; aggressiveness may be a problem in an urban, sedentary environment, but may have been necessary to survival in a less regulated society. It is easy to multiply such examples: the point to emphasize is that our genetical make-up is not *per se* all-determining. Rather, the person forged from those genes is inseparable from his or her history. The danger before all of us is failing to attain maturity because we have not exercised our ability to choose our environment.

physical body (Ps. 16:9; Pr. 14:30; Col. 2:11; *etc.*); Christ's view of adultery (Mt. 5:27–28) goes far beyond the legal definition of sexual intercourse. Scripture uses two words to describe the physical union of a man and a woman: *kollaō*, 'to join, glue or cement together', and *ginoskō*, 'to know'. The two words describe the very deep emotional and spiritual relationship between a man and a woman, the physical vehicle and sign of which is sexual intercourse. On a purely pragmatic level, contraception separates sex from procreation, but most Protestants interpret the 'one flesh' teaching as not prohibiting this.

The relevance of this digression into the nature of marriage is to elucidate the significance for a marriage of gametes from a third (and even a fourth) party, as happens when DI (donor insemination) or ovum donation (or both) takes place. DI has been ruled in a Scottish court not to be adultery (legally this was judged to involve physical union of a man and a woman), although to many it represents an illegitimate trespass into a marriage partnership. But, and this is the key in the present context, donor gametes are an unacceptable intrusion only if the genetic contribution has a major ethical importance. If genes are morally neutral (that is, if they have no more moral significance than, say, hair colour; this is the clear implication from our analysis of the constituents of our basic humanity; *cf.* p. 49; see also below, p. 73), donor gametes can have no intrinsic disruptive influence on a marriage. This does not prove that gamete donation is necessarily acceptable, but it means that it should not be rejected on the common ground that it involves adultery.

Consideration of marriage naturally leads on to consideration of families. Here we find biblical models surprisingly diverse. Carl Whitehouse (1983) has written:

Faced with the complex issue of what is involved in responsible parenthood, one turns to Scripture for guidance; one is then faced with the fact that, although there is a clear rule of lifelong marriage as the sole situation for sexual expression, there is less clarity on the right context for the rearing of children. As times one is amazed at the lack of condemnation of apparent aberrations. In Genesis we find a form of surrogate motherhood indulged in by the patriarchs; it may have been consistent with the social conventions of surrounding societies, but one is still surprised that it is not judged more harshly, for although Jacob's family had problems, the same can be said for strictly monogamous Isaac! Again, social parenting in Scripture was carried out on a more communal basis [than we are used to] and we do not consider

Hannah an irresponsible parent because Samuel was sent to the temple as soon as he was weaned. In some ways Scripture, and this is borne out in certain genealogies, holds the legal position of parent as of greater importance than the genetic . . .

Interestingly, sociological studies of children born following DI or IVF show that they are more contented and adjusted than children born following normal conception. There have not been many such studies because of the general secrecy around artificial insemination and the comparatively recent development of IVF, but all the evidence so far shows no sign that introduced genetic factors disrupt the children concerned or their family (Golombok *et al.* 1995).

All this leads us back to the fact that true humanness resides in God's image in us. Genes are important but not determinative (Medina 1991). The Hebrews did not have separate concepts of body and soul: Adam was created a 'man-soul', not a man with an injected soul. We tend to react against dualism, partly on the above ground, and partly as a response to the crudity of Cartesian dualism. But we need to beware of following theological fashions. For example, Blocher (1983:84) has pointed out that

. . . duality stands out unambiguously in the New Testament, just as it does in the Judaism of that era . . . it is presupposed by the doctrine of the survival of the soul/spirit without the body in the period between death and the final resurrection (1 Cor. 15:42ff.). But even in the Old Testament, despite the haziness of the concepts and the differing meanings that words have, it would be wrong to suppose that it was absent. The idea of an inner life is often expressed, with the help, amongst other things, of the concept of the heart.

Moule (1965–6) has argued that Paul's basic dualism is between disobedience and filial obedience, rather than between body and spirit. This has an interesting parallel with the interpretation given above (p. 49) that the image of God in human beings is about relationships, and confirms that the fall should be interpreted as primarily about a break in the relationships of God, humanity and nature. The physical structure of the body is not irrevocably linked with God's presence in that body.

So where does this leave us? My own belief is that the evidence is against the proposition that life begins at conception. Rogerson (1985:85) has concluded that

. . . even if we assume that the 'image' is asserting something ontological about mankind, what we do not know is whether the 'image' (whatever it is) is present from the moment of conception or whether, in Old Testament terms, it is there only after the 'unformed substance' has reached its definite human form . . . Nothing in the Bible clearly shows that the image of God is 'present' from the moment of conception.

Like Jerome and Augustine, I also want to be agnostic about the point at which God's image is impressed on the physical nature. The British legislation permits experimentation up to the time of formation of the primitive streak (two weeks after fertilization), which is when the embryo changes from an amorphous ball of cells to an organism with top and bottom, front and back. Other possibilities for 'ensoulment' (to use the old, inadequate term), are when the heart starts beating, or when the neural net is established and nerve impulses are detectable (this would be brain 'birth', parallel to brain 'death', which is a generally accepted definition of death).

I believe that we need to continue discussion about the 'beginning' of life. It has important consequences not merely for reproductive medicine, but also for a better understanding of a whole range of problems in bioethics (Dyson 1995). The essential point I want to underline is that the assumption that life begins at conception is no more than an assumption. We need to read the books of nature and of Scripture together and critically examine all relevant traditions. Only then will we be faithful to our calling as 'fully human' beings.

The right way forward would seem to be to acknowledge God's sovereignty over all life; to agree that his image in us places a definite limitation on the extent to which we may manipulate human material; but at the same time to accept that he expects us to use the skills we are given for proper ends, such as research on the causes of malformation and handicap. Only if we take an absolutist position like that of Paul Ramsey (1975 and elsewhere), who demands that any procedure must involve no risk whatsoever to an unconsenting child, can we decide differently with integrity.

The Human Fertilization and Embryology Act

It may be helpful to describe something of the working of the British legislation that followed the Warnock Report. There was considerable antagonism to the latter when it was published (*q.v.*, p. 67), particularly from 'pro-life' groups, and it was not clear to the Government how to proceed. Clearly some action was necessary, because DI and IVF and their practitioners were effectively unregulated. In the end, Parliament approved a law setting out the conditions for clinics carrying out DI, IVF and related procedures, allowing research on embryos up to fourteen days after the mixing of egg and sperm, but banning controversial research such as cloning by nuclear substitution or the creation of hybrids; requiring all couples to be offered counselling before treatment, and imposing a duty to consider the welfare of any child who might be born or who might be affected, before treatment goes ahead; making surrogacy agreements unenforceable in the courts; and setting up a statutory Authority to oversee centres, grant licences and advise the Government as required. (Full descriptions of the background and legislation are given by Morgan & Lee 1991, and Gunning & English 1993.)

The key factor in this was to be a Human Fertilization and Embryology Authority (HFEA). Constraints on membership were laid down: the members (appointed by the Ministers of Health) were to have lay people in the majority, and to be chaired by a lay person.

I am a member of the Authority. We have been in operation since 1991, and currently (1996) license just over 100 clinics for IVF and/or DI, and around forty research projects which have to satisfy one or more of five criteria: to further progress in the treatment of infertility; to increase knowledge about the causes of congenital disease or of miscarriages; to develop more effective techniques of contraception; or to develop methods for detecting the presence of gene or chromosome abnormalities in embryos before implantation. There is no doubt that the licensing role of the Authority has been important in increasing good clinical and technical practice, and in discouraging bad practices, by its ability to refuse, or to place conditions on, licences.

Licensing forms the bulk of the Authority's work, but an arguably more important role has been its function to stimulate and co-ordinate debate on ethical matters, and specifically to advise Government about the need for new laws and regulations.[4] Issues that have arisen in which the Authority has been involved include surrogacy, sex selection, fertility

[4] The first duty of the Authority as described in the Act is 'to keep under review information about embryos and any subsequent development'.

treatment for post-menopausal women, cloning (nuclear replacement is forbidden by law, but not dividing whole early embryos), freezing of embryos, the payment of egg or sperm donors, and others. One that raised particular interest was whether ova cultured from the ovaries of young women or even foetuses can be used for donation, either in research or in treatment. The question arose because the number of ova decrease rapidly during the life of a woman, and in theory many eggs could be obtained for donation from the ovaries of pre-menarchical women. This raises scientific issues about the safety of eggs, since many of the chromosomal defects that cause early foetal loss are maternal in origin. But more important were ethical issues – about the nature of donation, consent, the effect on the child born, the use of aborted tissue (and the fear that women might be pressurized to have an abortion because of the 'value' of the abortus), and others. The HFEA produced a consultation document setting out the issues and asking specific questions. Twenty-five thousand copies of the document were distributed, many to people requesting it following media coverage. Over 9,000 replies were received, many making detailed and well-thought-out points, although a fifth set out points made in campaign literature produced by anti-abortion groups rather than answering the questions posed in the document.

About 10% of respondents were in favour of using donated ovarian tissue in embryo research and infertility treatment, and just under 30% were against it. Some of those who approved the use said that a child was a gift from God however it was achieved, and that medical and scientific advances were evidence of God working through humankind; some who objected argued that children were a gift from God, and producing children by assisted means was 'against nature'. John Habgood, Archbishop of York, commented (*The Independent*, 11 January 1994) that 'from a theological perspective I would want to claim that our identity lies in the mind of God'. This is essentially the same point that I have made several times: that the crucial part of our true humanness is God's image in us (pp. 48, 76). He went on: 'But the givenness of our genetic inheritance is also basic to what we are, just as our bodies are, and our parents.' This is really the heart of the debate. Personally I have no doubt that God wants us to be responsible managers of our biology and that we are failing him if we draw back from his trust in us (Gn. 1:26). I return to this theme in the next chapter (p. 95). But how much should we defer to our 'genetic inheritance'? The answer to this question can only be that our identity in God's mind must be allowed to control; to suppress 'this treasure in jars of clay' (2 Cor. 4:7) in favour of our animalness must be close to being the sin against the Holy Spirit.

At the end of the Consultation, the HFEA, having analysed all the responses made to it but making its own decision (ethics cannot – or should not – be decided by referendum), concluded that for infertility treatment

> . . . different considerations apply to the use of ovarian tissue from the three sources discussed: live donors, cadavers and foetuses. Balancing benefits against risk of harm . . . it would be acceptable to use ovarian tissue only from live donors. While the Authority has no objection in principle to the use in infertility treatment of cadaveric ovarian tissue from adult women it will not currently approve its use. The Authority does not consider the use of foetal ovarian tissue in treatment to be acceptable . . . [but] in the case of embryo research, the use of ovarian tissue from all three sources to produce embryos (which cannot in law be inserted into the womb of a living woman) is acceptable.

The HFEA document continues:

> It is in the nature of human beings to try to shape their world. Medical treatment is by definition interventionist and has been developed through research and practice to overcome problems which afflict and distress men and women. Few would argue against interfering in the natural order for the purpose of healing, but some people have reservations about intervention in order to relieve infertility . . .

This is the crux of the dilemma; how far can or should we intervene? Intervention in genetical matters is sometimes condemned as 'playing God'. If the motive is merely to 'play', this is properly suspect. But God has specifically commanded us to 'have dominion' over natural processes and condemned those who failed to do this (for instance, in the teaching of the parables of the talents and of the wicked husbandmen: Mt. 25:14–30; 21:33–44). The limits of intervention have to be determined, I believe, but there is no easy answer as to what they should be; there is no simple, clear-cut solution.

Conclusions

The classical Christian approach to ethical questions has been through the concept of natural law, based on Romans 2:14–15: 'When Gentiles . . . do by nature things required by the law, they are [have] a law [that is, in contrast and addition to that which was revealed to Moses and the prophets and recorded in the books of the Old Testament] for themselves . . . since they show that the requirements of the law are written in their hearts, their consciences also bearing witness, and their thoughts now accusing, now even defending them . . .' The concept has roots also in Stoic and Aristotelian ethics. In other words, it is assumed to be possible to discern by reason (and conscience) the laws by which human beings should live. Moreover, it is claimed that such laws are universal, although they may need clarification through revelation and reinforcement through specifically Christian teaching.[5] On this view, intervention is permissible on two grounds: (1) *the principle of totality*, so that (for example) a diseased organ may be removed or modified if its malfunction constitutes a serious threat to the whole; or (2) *the principle of double effect*, whereby an action is not forbidden even if one of its consequences is bad, so long as its overall aim is good. On these principles, it is possible to argue that infertility is a harm which can be legitimately alleviated since to do so would result in the good of a family. Thus even on the classical axioms (commonly expressed by saying that some practice 'is not natural'), modern developments described in this chapter can be accepted as good, or even necessary.

Are there other considerations which we must take into account? How do we discover the mind of God in matters which were completely outside the experience and imagination of the biblical authors? Ultimately decisions have to be made responsibly on all the information available. Nowhere are we told in the Bible that life is sacred; nowhere are we told that life begins at conception. We are faced with new

---

[5] Michael Coghlan (1990) has argued that recent Roman Catholic teaching, particularly the Vatican *Instruction on Respect for Human Life in its Origin and on the Dignity of Procreation* (1987) (which is an elaboration of part of *Humanae Vitae*), violates this principle, and hence deviates from traditional teaching, which was assumed to apply to all humankind. Coghlan concludes that 'the Vatican's teaching on the status of the human embryo rests on flawed rational arguments, bolstered by religious presuppositions'.

questions as a result of technical developments. We should not fear the developments, but use them as tools to further God's purposes (Nelson 1994). The practical question is how to discover what those purposes are for oneself or for society. Once we assume that we are autonomous beings, genetic and reproductive intervention quickly assumes manipulatory possibilities. In contrast, when we acknowledge that we are the handiwork of God who creates and redeems, such intervention becomes a means by which God can alleviate some of our suffering and anguish. This is why the nature of humanness is of paramount importance in this debate (A. C. Berry 1987, 1993).

I end with what we can call the conundrum of non-existence (Jones 1991, 1994). Think of a couple with two children, who had agreed that they had 'completed' their family; however, they then decide to have two more. These later ones come into existence only because the couple changed their minds. Parents can choose to bring or not to bring children into the world, and to act as co-creators with God. We agonize over the morality of artificial reproduction, but seldom stand back and review the awe-ful decisions we make, or fail to make, when children are conceived in the standard way.

Think now of the ways by which the non-existence of the two children might have been accomplished: by abstinence, or by various forms of contraception including the prevention of implantation of the fertilized ovum. Is there any moral difference between these methods, since the end result is that the children do not exist, and the parents are totally unaware as to whether or not fertilization ever occurred? For the parents, the crucial decision is whether or not they will bring another person into the world, and it is this decision that involves them.

Summing up: Scripture does not give such clear-cut teaching as many assume on how we should value the very early embryo. Biology shows the pre-implantation embryo to have the potential to travel down a number of different developmental pathways. Only a small number of the cells which arise from the original fertilized egg are destined to become the embryo itself; and there is a high wastage rate of whole embryos, all giving an impression of imprecision and prodigality. The loss of these early pre-implantation embryos, whose presence remains unknown to anybody, can in no way be compared with the loss of beloved children through famine, or even loss through miscarriage. Both of these have an impact on parents.

At implantation the embryo establishes a relationship with the mother and becomes valued by her. Perhaps we can take up this clue, and, like the mother, afford the embryo little intrinsic value prior to implantation. After this, with increasing growth and development its status increases for both the mother and her attendants. But when is the image of God fully present? At what point does the embryo become my neighbour for whom Christ died? Is this a gradual process or a decisive moment? There are many of these questions, and it is only honest to admit that we have only tentative answers to most of them. This whole area, I believe, is one for prayerful discussion; dogmatic confrontation is unhelpful, and indeed dangerous if it is based on wrong premises.

5

ENVIRONMENTAL ETHICS

A major change in the way we view the world has taken place in the last couple of decades. In the words of the United Kingdom's statement of its national environmental strategy (*This Common Inheritance*, 1990):

> Ever since the Age of Enlightenment, we have had an almost boundless faith in our own intelligence and in the benign consequences of our actions. Whatever the discoveries of science, whatever the rate at which we multiplied as a species, whatever the changes we made to our seas and landscape, we have believed that the world would stay much the same in all its fundamentals. We now know that this is no longer true. This perception could have consequences for national action and international diplomacy as far-reaching as those which resulted from the splitting of the atom . . . We may not be seeing the end of Nature. But Nature is certainly under threat.

Interestingly, the Government's reaction to this diagnosis was a moral one. Their strategy continues:

> The starting point for this Government is the ethical imperative of stewardship which must underlie all environmental policies. Mankind has always been capable of great good and evil. This is certainly true of our role as custodians of our planet. The Government's approach begins with the recognition that it is mankind's duty to look after our world prudently and conscientiously . . . We have a moral duty to look after our planet and to hand it on in good order to future generations.

This assertion was explicitly reaffirmed in the British Government's commitments at the Rio Summit of 1992 (the United Nations Conference on Environment and Development), which are spelt out in detail in a second policy document, *Sustainable Development* (1994).

Politicians use moral language as part of their normal repartee, but it is highly unusual for official pronouncements to stray beyond specific commitments to action (or inaction). Is there anything that distinguishes policy on the environment from that on, say, health, housing or education? The proper answer is that nothing should distinguish it: honourable government should be trustworthy and responsible at all levels and on all subjects. One *reason* the environment has emerged as a moral issue may be that the complexity of environmental pathways means that the consequences of human actions may often be far removed in time and space from their causes; when this strikes home, the cumulative reaction can be distressing and compelling. It is not intuitively obvious (and therefore all the more shaming) that pollution from *my* local power station may be killing fish and trees hundreds of miles away, or that *my* fridge or air conditioning is destroying the ozone layer tens of miles above the earth and causing cancers in another continent. Consequently, many of the environmental actions which are needed are essentially altruistic, in that they do not help me (or my constituents) at all. Indeed, they may actually cause me inconvenience or cost, and help people I have never met and with whom I have no obvious connection. But even though politicians tend to avoid penalizing their own constituents – they scream loudly when others damage our environment, such as by over-fishing our seas or polluting our pastures with radioactive fallout – they are forced into action by public outcry when supported by rational persuasion, helped a little by moral courage (Ashby 1993).

The reality is that political boundaries at all levels (local, regional and national) are irrelevant to most important environmental pathways. We can damage our environment either by sophisticated assaults on it (ironically, often as a consequence of insulating ourselves from our natural surroundings) or by the sheer pressure of human numbers on basic resources such as firewood or cultivatable land. And our awareness of such damage is both recent and patchy.

Dealing with environmental concern

The change in our perception of environmental resilience comes from the recognition that global stresses are appearing, and at an ever-increasing rate. For centuries we have battled with local difficulties. China has had nearly 2,000 famines within its borders in the last 2,000 years; the decline of the Babylonian grain-growing culture was probably due to declining soil fertility as salinity built up in an over-extended irrigation system; Seneca was repeatedly advised by his doctor to leave Rome, and immediately felt better when he at last moved away from the city's fumes and cooking smells. The earliest recorded air pollution incident in Britain was in 1257, when Henry III's queen, Eleanor, evacuated Nottingham Castle because of coal smoke. Three and a half centuries later, James I was 'moved with compassion for the decayed fabric of [old] St Paul's Cathedral near approaching ruin by the corroding quality of coal smoke to which it had long been subjected', and a few years later John Evelyn wrote a tract on air pollution (*Fumigium, or the Inconvenience of the Aer and Smoak of London Dissipated*, 1661), in which he described

> . . . that Hellish and dismall cloud of SEA-COALE perpetually imminent over London . . . which is so universally mixed with the otherwise wholesome and excellent Aer, that her Inhabitants breath nothing but an impure and thick Mist, accompanied with a fuliginous and filthy vapour, which renders them obnoxious to a thousand inconveniences, corrupting the Lungs and disordering the entire habit of their Bodies; so that Catharrs, Phthisicks, Coughs and Consumptions rage more in this one city than in the whole Earth besides.

Such examples can be continued almost indefinitely. Sicily was once the 'granary of Italy', but less and less corn is grown there as the soil deteriorates under excessive cultivation and the grazing of goats; the Scottish Highlands are a man-made wet desert; the dust bowl of the southern central United States arose from the practice of cultivation in an area where the rainfall is low and the soil susceptible to erosion by wind and storm; and so on. But all these are geographically limited disasters. The new situation in which we find ourselves involves calamities outside our own locality and control: persistent pesticides throughout the world's food chains, ionizing radiation ignorant and intolerant of political boundaries, ozone holes 20 miles above our heads, oxides of nitrogen and sulphur destroying freshwater life and trees far from their source, and global warming potentially changing the distribution of animals and plants over whole continents. And all this in a context where the major disturbing factor – the human species – is increasing at a rate of 180 people a minute and will, we are told, double to a total of 11 billion in under a century's time.

In his novel *On the Beach* (1957), Nevil Shute described the varied reactions of Australians faced with an inexorable rise in radiation following a nuclear war in the northern hemisphere. Some carried on as normal; some responded like the Stoics or Epicureans of old, resigning themselves to the inevitable or flinging themselves into hedonistic frenzy; others 'flipped', becoming shrill and unreasonable; a few sought solace in religion. Shute's book is a parable for our times as we face environmental dangers. Like Shute's Australians, we cannot escape. Our ancestors could move to the next valley or the next county, or emigrate to under-populated lands (as did the Beaker Folk in the mid-second millennium BC or the Vikings in the seventh and eighth centuries AD), or to the Americas as in the seventeenth and eighteenth centuries. We now have nowhere to go. The world is full. A new spectre is millions of environmental refugees fleeing into already crowded countries, their numbers completely overwhelming border controls or planned quotas or the like. Whether our image is of 'spaceship Earth' or a 'sinking ark', the stark fact is that we are running out of world.

The 1950s and 1960s saw a progressive increase in environmental concern, which in Britain reached a peak with the 'Countryside in 1970' conferences under the impetus of the Duke of Edinburgh, involving the leaders of nearly all the national environmental groups, representatives of farming and landowning interests, and key industrialists and government officials. A major concern at the time was the industrialization of agriculture and the increasing human pressure on the countryside; measures to conserve wildlife populations could no longer be confined to nature reserves.

The conferences raised consciousness of environmental problems to a new level. During the same period Rachel Carson (1962) drew attention to the insidious dangers of persistent pesticides in her book *Silent Spring*. It is worth recording that British research was at least as advanced as that in Rachel Carson's North America; as Norman Moore (1987) has elegantly expounded, Monks Wood Experimental Station was opened in 1961 with a remit in part to investigate the ecological effects of pesticides. In 1967 the wreck of the Liberian oil tanker *Torrey Canyon* off Land's End alerted the British public in a vivid way to the ever-present risks of oil pollution. The Church of England made its contribution with a Church Assembly debate on a Working Party Report, *Man in His Living Environment* (1969), which declared that 'despoiling the earth is a blasphemy and not just an error of judgment . . . The situation which is created by men's abuse of his power is not God's intention. The deadly sins of avarice, greed, pride destroy the earth. Dust bowls, deserts and a poisoned environment are the consequences.'

In 1972 a computer simulation carried out at Massachusetts Institute of Technology was published under the title *The Limits to Growth* (Meadows *et al*. 1972). Its message was that the economic and industrial systems of affluent countries would collapse around the year 2100 unless two correctives were taken: that birth rate should equal death rate, and that capital investment should equal capital depreciation. If these conditions were met, a 'stabilized world model' could result. The authors have recently (1992) rerun their model with additional data, and confirmed their earlier prediction, with the ominous addition that, if no constraints are applied, there will be an overshoot in resource misuse, which would exacerbate the subsequent collapse.

The MIT model was taken as the basis for a 'Blueprint for Survival', issued in the *Ecologist* magazine in 1972, and endorsed by a group of leading ecologists. Its argument was that the non-renewable resources which provide the raw materials and energy sources for much of industry are threatened with drastic depletion within a time-span that ordinarily commands politicians' attention, as a result of exponential increase in consumption and of population growth; and the waste which accompanies this exploitation threatens the processes which sustain human life. The authors of the Blueprint proposed a radical reordering of priorities, with industrial societies converting themselves into stable communities characterized by minimum disruption of ecological processes, maximum conservation of materials and energy, and static populations. *The Times* of London headed its first leader on 14 January 1972, 'The prophets may be right'.

But the calculations of *The Limits to Growth* and the Blueprint were rendered void within a few years by the Arab–Israeli wars and a massive increase in the price of fossil fuels. Lord Ashby (who had been first Chairman of the Royal Commission on Environmental Pollution, which was set up in 1970 and remains the only standing Royal Commission in Britain concerned with scientific issues) took *A Second Look at Doom* in 1975, speaking of the ominous instability of manmade ecosystems. He warned that 'if we experience a shift in the balance of economic power between nations which own resources and nations which need those resources to keep their economies going, one sure consequence would be an increase in tension in the social systems on both sides . . . The tempting way to resolve these tensions is by autocracy and force.' In other words, the period of good-mannered agreement over the use of resources was probably over. Conservation was on the international agenda, but it would be nothing more than a desirable dream unless there were a change of attitudes as well as intellectual assent to impending problems (Brenton 1994).

1980 onwards

The consensus of the 1970s was destroyed by the disappearance of the myth of cheap energy and the realization that the issues at stake were too fundamental to be dealt with merely by acknowledging that justice was needed in the use of scarce resources. In North America, the breakdown of the consensus has been obscured by the persisting low price of fossil fuel. This is storing up long-term problems, because the problems agonized over in the 'Countryside in 1970' conferences were (and are) still with us. In 1980 a 'World Conservation Strategy' (WCS) was produced by the International Union for the Conservation of Nature, the World Wildlife Fund (now the Worldwide Fund for Nature) and the United Nations Environmental Programme. It was an unashamedly utilitarian document, stressing that every aspect of human activity benefits from conservation (and conversely, is as likely to be hindered by environmental mismanagement), and that therefore we have a vested interest in looking after our environment. Implicit in it was the concept of 'sustainable development', a theme taken up and expanded in *Our Common Future*, the Report of the World Commission on Environment and Development (1987), the 'Brundtland Report'.

The stated aim of the WCS was (1) to maintain essential ecological processes and life-support systems; (2) to preserve genetic diversity; and (3) to ensure the sustainable utilization of species and ecosystems. The achievement of this aim was assumed to be inevitable, once the problem and possible solutions were defined. This was a major fallacy; right decisions do not automatically spring from accurate knowledge.[1] This is

---

[1] Although the science is different, the frustration of Albert Einstein (in an address to the National Commission of Nuclear Scientists, May 1946) is the same: 'The release of atom power has changed everything except our way of thinking and thus we are being

vividly illustrated by the history of clean-air legislation. The association between air pollution and death rates was established by John Graunt as early as the mid-seventeenth century. During the nineteenth century there were repeated attempts to pass clean-air laws in the UK Parliament, but it was not until a major London smog in 1952 led to the abandonment of *La Traviata* at Sadlers Wells and the collapse of prize cattle at the Smithfield Show that comprehensive smoke-control legislation was passed. (An excellent account of the political equivocation on this issue is given by Ashby & Anderson 1981.)

The Strategy, being in part a UN document, required responses from member nations of UNEP. The UK response was composed of reports from seven groups, dealing with industry, city, countryside, marine and coastal issues, international policy, education, and ethics (*The Conservation and Development Programme for the UK*, 1983). The originality in this exercise was the setting up of a group on ethics. Ethics is mentioned only once in the WCS, without elaboration or justification: 'A new ethic, embracing plants and animals as well as people, is required for human societies to live in harmony with the natural world on which they depend for survival and well-being.' This indifference was criticized at a conference held in Ottawa in 1986 to review progress in implementing the strategy, and it was resolved to include ethics in any revision of the Strategy. The updated strategy (published as *Caring for the Earth*, 1991) does indeed take on board this recommendation (Engel 1993).

The task of the UK ethics group was to put forward practical proposals about the shaping of sensible attitudes towards the environment in the multidisciplinary no-man's-land where philosophy, psychology, politics, biology and economics meet. The group dealing with education called its report *Education for Commitment*, but something more was needed. I was commissioned to produce the Ethics Report, guided by a Review Group chaired by Lord Ashby and appointed by a national co-ordinating committee.

The Review Group met only once. It was split, apparently irrevocably, between managers and those who regarded our environmental plight as wholly the fault of human incompetence and arrogance. At the time it seemed pointless to pursue this debate. I developed an aphorism that 'we

---

driven unarmed towards a catastrophe . . . The solution of this problem lies in the heart of humankind.'

are both a part of nature and apart from nature'. This formed part of our Report, which was written by me with considerable help from Lord Ashby and individual discussion with other members of the group. It would be good to think that this aphorism (or rather, the truth on which it is based) helped to defuse the polarization in environmental attitudes, at least in the UK where environmental debates have been much more rational and less confrontational than in some countries. The realization that sensible environmental actions do not need full agreement on the underlying premises is now gaining ground, but such pragmatic co-operation will always be fragile and liable to failure through challenge of its determining motives.

The Ethics Section of the UK Response to the WCS began with an examination of the factors that determine attitudes, which is where the need for ethics came in; not as a branch of academic philosophy, but in the fundamental sense as an expression of moral understanding 'usually in the form of guidelines or rules of conduct, involving evaluations of value or worth'.

Value was a key concept, but determining value in the environmental sense is confusing, as at least four different criteria can be applied: (1) cost in the market-place, quantified as money; (2) usefulness for individuals or society; (3) intrinsic worth, which depends on the objective quality of the object valued, in contrast to the market-place cost (which is quantifiable only in relation to the price of other things that can be acquired in its place); and (4) symbolic or conceptual, such as a national flag or liberty.

These four meanings can change independently for the same object. For example, similar volumes of water in a river in highland Scotland or lowland England may be assigned different values by an economist according to whether it is drunk, fished or treated as an amenity; an object of beauty or a stinking sewer; a boundary between counties or countries; a barrier to the spread of pests; and so on.

Now, our interest in, and therefore valuation of, the environment relates to ourselves, our community, and future generations, but nature itself also has its own interest in survival and health. The first three of these interests are clearly anthropocentric; they are the basis of the 1980 World Conservation Strategy. Although they may conflict with each other, in principle some accommodation is usually possible. Considerable advance has been made in recent years by economists recognizing that proper accounting involves taking note of both non-material and trans-generational values (Sagoff 1988).

Nature's intrinsic worth is more difficult to justify. The commonest rationalization is explicitly utilitarian: we should preserve as many species as possible in case they are useful to us humans (for instance, as a source of anti-cancer drugs, or the elusive elixir of eternal youth). Ashby (1978) has argued that we should learn to value a landscape or biological mechanism in the same way that we are prepared to protect and pay for human artifacts like buildings or paintings. Bryan Norton (1987), an American philosopher, has developed a 'weakly anthropocentric' approach, based on the proposition that we are continually being transformed by our contact with the world around us, which is therefore an integral part of our human development.

The difficulty about defining the intrinsic worth of nature led the Church of England to produce *Our Responsibility for the Living Environment* (1986), a follow-on to its 1969 Report. This was originally intended as a theological reflection on the ethics in the UK Response to the WCS, although its final form was rather wider. Its core was that we live in a world created, redeemed and sustained by God; since this is God's world, not ours, it has intrinsic worth. Interestingly (and encouragingly), the implication (although perhaps not the theology) of this point was taken up in the UK Government White Paper on the environment, *This Common Inheritance*, already quoted. Citing the then Prime Minister Mrs Thatcher (who, in turn, drew upon John Ruskin), the White Paper affirmed that 'we do not hold a freehold on our world, but only a full repairing lease. We have a moral duty to look after our planet and to hand it on in good order to future generations.' Prime Minister John Major used very similar words in his speech to the Earth Summit in Rio.

Perceived failures

The idea that we are running out of world is commonly expressed as a vague but compelling worry that 'something is wrong', and that while science has failed to deal fairly and adequately with human needs, religion is perceived as either too personal or too remote to cope with the real complexities of twentieth-century life.

What is the way forward? We can agree there is a problem, but there is certainly no generally accepted solution. There is a common belief that the Judeo-Christian tradition, from which western science and technology sprang, has been one of the main problems, because, in the words of Ian McHarg (1969),

If one seeks licence for those who would increase radioactivity, create canals and harbours with atomic bombs, employ poisons without constraint, or give consent to the bulldozer mentality, there could be no better injunction than [Genesis 1:28: 'God blessed them (the newly formed human beings) and said to them, "Be fruitful and increase in number; fill the earth and subdue it. Rule over the fish of the sea and the birds of the air and over every living creature that moves on the ground" '] . . . Dominion and subjugation must be expunged as the biblical injunction of man's relation to nature.

In Max Nicholson's words (1970), 'the first step must be plainly to reject and to scrub out the complacent image of Man the Conqueror of Nature, and of Man Licensed by God to conduct himself as the earth's worse pest'.

The most frequently quoted indictment of Christianity is that of the American historian Lynn White (1967), who declared in a lecture to the American Association for the Advancement of Science that 'Christianity . . . insisted that it is God's will that man exploit nature for his proper ends . . . Christianity bears a huge burden of guilt'. White's thesis was based on the premise that our increasing ability to control and harness natural forces was flawed by the assumption that 'we are superior to nature, contemptuous of it, willing to use it for our slightest whim . . . We shall continue to have a worsening ecological crisis until we reject the Christian axiom that nature has no reason for existence but to serve man . . . Both our present science and our present technology are so tinctured with orthodox Christian arrogance towards nature that no solution for our ecologic crisis can be expected from them alone.' But, and this is a key inference, 'since the roots of our trouble are so largely religious, the remedy must be essentially religous, whether we call it that or not'. White went on to conclude that our main hope should be a refocused Christianity, not a wholesale repudiation of it; he suggested that we should return to the 'alternative Christian view of nature and man's relation to it', exemplified by Francis of Assisi's respect for the living world (Schaeffer 1970). He proposed Francis as a patron saint for ecologists; in 1980 Pope John Paul II accepted the idea.

The malignant effects of Judeo-Christianity can, however, be over-stressed. Running parallel to the 'dominance' tradition is an equally strong stewardship theme (Attfield 1983). Indeed, stewardship has been a significant key to the Christian attitude to nature for most of the church's history. It was implicit in the Celtic church of the Dark Ages, and is explicit in the Benedictine Rule, which was a major influence shaping society in the Middle Ages (De Waal 1984). It is a doctrinal corrective to unfettered human dominance on two grounds: (1) God's command in Genesis was in the context of human beings created 'in his image', which involves trustworthiness and responsibility; (2) Hebrew kingship was meant to be a servant-kingship, exemplified by the instructions given to David and Solomon and ideally shown by Jesus Christ; it was not a despotic potency.

The Bible doctrine of conservation is straightforward. It has three elements: (1) we live in God's world; (2) he has entrusted it to us to look after; and (3) we will be held responsible for our stewardship of it. (A number of excellent Christian books on the environment have appeared in recent years, including Granberg-Michaelson 1987; L. Wilkinson 1991; Elsdon 1992; Osborn 1993).

In fact the dominant theme in the Bible is not stewardship, but the whole creation praising God. This comes out repeatedly in the Psalms, in the final chapter of Job, and in the messianic passages of Isaiah. The outworking of this in the Old Testament is a strong land ethic (C. J. H. Wright 1990). In modern times, a land ethic is particularly associated with the writings of Aldo Leopold. He wrote that we must 'quit thinking about decent land use as solely an economic problem. Examine each question in terms of what is ethically and aesthetically right, as well as what is economically expedient. A thing is right when it tends to preserve the integrity, stability and beauty of the biotic community. It is wrong when it tends otherwise' (Leopold 1949:224–225). Unfortunately, many green religionists have interpreted 'a land ethic' as a call to preservation, rather than to responsible management. The prophet of this approach is John Muir, who rejected his Christian upbringing and claimed to have found most empathy in Buddhism (Austin 1987).

The New Testament also contains much that is relevant to our care for the world, in particular the teaching that nature has been redeemed by Christ's work. The danger of nature separate from God is that it becomes treated as a mere 'thing', neutral or even disordered and needing to be quelled (Bratton 1983). In so far as they had a theology, this was the attitude of the post-Enlightenment Romantics; nature had to be tamed and tidied. This is not the Bible's teaching. Creation is described as 'good' because it is in covenant with the Creator (Heb. 1:1–2).

In the Old Testament, God is understood as absolutely transcendent and the world as non-divine. This de-divinization of nature is a basic premise or prime requisite, for technology and political and social progress. However, de-divinization, as such, tends to lead to de-personalization. This tendency is overcome in the New Testament. In the theologies of John and Paul, God's transcendence is still maintained, although he is now understood in a personalistic way, as personalized in Christ. This personalization of the world in Jesus Christ is particularly marked in the writings of Paul (Eph. 1:9, 10, 22, 23; Col. 1:15–20; Phil. 2:5; Rom. 8:18–25) (Faricy 1982:7; see also De Witt 1991).

This is not to deny that the plundering attitudes condemned by McHarg and Nicholson have been uncommon. To some extent they can be traced to rationalization by farmers and land managers of their increasing success over 'nature' as technology developed. But the fact that the biblical teaching on dominion was frequently misinterpreted should not be allowed to usurp its correct interpretation, or we should still be believing in a geocentric universe (despite Galileo) or a creation week in 4004 BC (despite Lyell and Darwin).

Furthermore, the habit of blaming Christianity for all our environmental disasters is wrong; a quick survey shows that environmental degradation is almost universal whenever excessive strain is put on natural systems. Leaving aside the horrors produced in Eastern Europe under specifically anti-religious regimes, in other places over-grazing, deforestation and the like on a scale sufficient to destroy civilization have been committed by Egyptians, Assyrians, Romans, North Africans, Persians, Indians, Aztecs, Mayans and Buddhists. Japan has pollution problems as bad as anywhere in the world. Former European Commission President Jacques Delors has commented, 'I have to say that the Oriental religions have failed to prevent to any marked degree the appropriation of the natural environment . . . Despite different traditions, the right to use or exploit nature seems to have found in industrial countries the same economic justification.'

Green religion

Perhaps in response to all these failures, there has been a trend in recent years to develop various forms of eco-religion, sometimes based on established faiths, but more often on an eccentric ragbag of beliefs. The problems of uncontrolled eclectism are illustrated by the fate of the 'Assisi Declarations' produced by some of the major world faiths (Buddhism, Christianity, Hinduism, Islam, Judaism and Baha'i) at the twenty-fifth anniversary celebration of the Worldwide Fund for Nature in 1986. These innocuous and laudable statements led to the establishment of an international 'Network of Conservation and Religion', a useful initiative. But attempts to further the aims of bringing together conservation and religion have led to some highly contentious activities, such as cathedral creation celebrations involving wholly incompatible philosophies, with joint worship by people of different religions, improperly joining different faiths, including monotheists and polytheists. For example, the Coventry celebration in 1988 included a prayer which ran: 'Our brothers and sisters of the creation, the mighty trees, the broad oceans, the air, the earth, the creatures of creation, forgive us and reconcile us to you.' Such heterodoxy stimulated in 1991 an open letter which was signed by over 2,000 Church of England clergy, and which stated:

> We desire to love and respect people of other faiths. We respect their rights and freedoms. We wholeheartedly support cooperation in appropriate community, social, moral and political issues between Christians and those of other faiths wherever this is possible . . . [but] We are deeply concerned about gatherings for interfaith worship and prayer involving Christian people . . . We believe these events, however motivated, conflict with the Christian duty to proclaim the Gospel. They imply that salvation is offered by God not only through Jesus Christ but by other means and thus deny his uniqueness and finality as the only Saviour.

More insidious and difficult to confront are the beliefs underlying the so-called New Age movement. The term 'New Age' has no precise meaning, but the movement is portrayed by its adherents as a sign of the time when the world is moving from Pisces, dominated by Christianity, to Aquarius, symbolizing unity. Such a faith (if that is an appropriate description) is explicitly pantheistic and relativistic (since there are no distinctions between right and wrong); salvation is achieved through self-realization, so various human-potential movements are claimed by New Agers.

The present manifestation of the New Age derives from sundry utopianisms of the eighteenth and nineteenth centuries (especially the

Theosophical Society), but it has its immediate roots in the anti-authoritarianism of the 1960s, with its appeals to romanticism as an antidote to the presumed determinism of science. Whereas mainstream thought accepted the need for environmental management and statutory controls, the emerging green movement sought the removal of constraints, allowing life to be lived in harmony with the earth. Key concepts were balance, stability and peace. A seminal document was E. F. Schumacher's *Small is Beautiful* (1973) with its emphasis on appropriate or intermediate technology. Big business and central government are distrusted. Tradition and authority are suspect, although selectively endorsed in the guise of earth myths and native customs. Green religion tends to be a passionate animism.

Some of this is healthy. It is right to examine traditions, test authority and seek to improve the structures of society. But it is too easy to jettison truth in the course of rethinking, and the situation of eco-religion is complicated by the vast spectrum of beliefs and practices between the extreme greens and the most orthodox establishmentarians. Three foci within green religion are, however, worth mentioning.

The first of these is *creation spirituality*, as propounded by the former Roman Catholic priest, Matthew Fox (1983). Fox seeks to unite modern cosmology with 'traditional wisdoms', within which Fox includes his own background of Dominican mysticism; he frequently quotes medieval visionaries such as Hildegard of Bingen (1098–1179), Meister Eckart (1260–1329), Julian of Norwich (1342–1415) and Thomas Traherne (1636–74). He argues for the replacement of the so-called theology of redemption and fall by a creation-centred one, which he sees as an optimistic progression, as opposed to any acceptance of disorder and a need for redemption and reconciliation. For Fox, the biblical God is a sadistic 'fascist' deity; in his thinking, 'we are we and we are God'. Our divinity is awakened through ecstasy – drugs, sex, yoga, ritual drumming or Transcendental Meditation; 'the experience of ecstasy is the experience of God'. Crucifixion and resurrection are transferred from the historical Jesus to Mother Earth; Easter is the life, death and resurrection of Mother Earth, a constantly sacrificed paschal lamb. Fox's religion is one in which Christ becomes one among many players on the world's stage. Fox asserts a form of pantheism where everything is holy and therefore to be worshipped, although he insists that his God is bigger than the universe and that his faith is really panentheistic (meaning that God is in everything, but is more than everything). But this distinction between pantheism and panentheism is slight, and, as C. S. Lewis put it in *The Problem of Pain* (1962), 'Pantheism is a creed, not so much false as hopelessly behind the times. Once, before creation, it would have been true to say that everything was God. But God created; He caused things to be other than Himself.' (A detailed criticism of Fox's views is given by Brearley 1992.)

Fox's cosmic Christianity must be distinguished from the more conventional panentheism urged by the so-called process theologians (such as John Cobb and the biologist Charles Birch); this features in many World Council of Churches publications and has links with liberation theology (Birch *et al.* 1990). Process theology begins from the premise that God must be open to outside influences (such as tragedy, prayer and so on) and therefore open to change by the world he has made. He is therefore subject to happenings in time; past and present events become joined into a continuum, and redemption becomes part of this process. Consequently Christ's work is downplayed; process theology tends toward a unitarian faith, not a trinitarian one.

The second focus is the concept of *Gaia*. Many green religionists have taken hold of the scientific hypothesis propounded by James Lovelock in 1969 (a useful summary appears in Rambler *et al.* 1989), that the world and its atmosphere form a single self-regulating negative feedback system ('Gaia', after the Greek goddess of the earth). They use it as a justification for the incorporation of human life as merely one element in an interacting but unitary organism. This is not the place to discuss the correctness of the science; Gaia has been an excellent hypothesis in the technical scientific sense of stimulating research to validate or disprove it. The problem has been wild extrapolation from the basic concept, with the world being seen as a living creature who can be abused or propitiated; Gaia has become a divine entity to be worshipped as a goddess from whose womb we have come. In other words, Gaia science has been hijacked as an intellectual justification for pantheism.

It is not necessary, of course, to endue Gaia with metaphysical properties. Some Christians see the interconnectedness of organic and inorganic systems as an example of the 'anthropic principle', which says that there are too many 'coincidences' in the properties of natural systems for the world to have arisen by chance. In this sense, the anthropic principle becomes a restatement of the medieval argument from design for the existence of God (Montefiore 1985; Polkinghorne 1989).

The third focus within green religion is *deep ecology*. Some of the more important prophets of green religion are the American founders of the cult of wilderness, notably Henry David Thoreau and John Muir (Muir was born in Dunbar, Scotland, but was taken to Wisconsin in 1849 at the age of eleven). Muir was fond of religious language. For example, having just lost a battle to preserve a tract of wild land he wrote: 'These temple destroyers, devotees of ravaging commercialism, seem to have a perfect contempt for Nature, and instead of lifting their eyes to the God of the mountains, lift them to the Almighty Dollar.' The mantle of these early prophets then passed to Aldo Leopold, who turned the notion of respect for nature into a 'land ethic', complementing the ethics of relationships between individuals and with society. Leopold's ideas have in turn been extended by a number of contemporary philosophers, notably the Norwegian Arne Naess and the American Holmes Rolston III (for a review, see Brennan 1988). Naess contrasts what he calls shallow ecology (which to him merely deals with symptoms, such as fighting pollution and resource depletion) with deep ecology, based on 'biospheric egalitarianism' (meaning that all things have an equal right to life, although Naess allows self-defence against organisms threatening health or survival). For Naess, deep ecology should explicitly challenge and confront the superficialities of conventional scientific (shallow) ecology; he converges on the New Age position by seeing 'self-realization' as a core for fully understanding deep concepts. He believes that deep ecology begins to articulate a comprehensive worldview, linking 'people who ask "ecological questions" in Christianity, Taoism, Buddhism and Native American rituals' (Naess 1989).

The environmental complaint

Neither science nor religion by itself can produce a complete answer to our environmental problems (Oelschlaeger 1994). The toothlessness of science alone was recognized by the lack of impact of the World Conservation Strategy, which fell into the Enlightenment fallacy that knowledge automatically produces sensible responses; it was underlined by the calling forth of the Assisi Declarations by the Worldwide Fund for Nature and its support for a conservation and religion network; it was made explicit by the Duke of Edinburgh when setting up a consultation on Christianity and the environment, posing the question, 'There must be a moral as well as a practical argument for environmental conservation. What is it?' (Duke of Edinburgh & Mann 1989). The confusions of religion are illustrated by uncertainties about whether to preserve or manage; about the role of established faiths or traditions; and by the selective misuse of scientific data.

Karl Popper has written, 'The fact that science cannot make any pronouncement about ethical principles has been misinterpreted as indicating that there are no such principles, while in fact the search for truth presupposes ethics.' Is it possible to produce a generally acceptable environmental ethic? The answer to this must be 'Yes'. In 1989, the Economic Summit Nations (the G7) called a conference on environmental ethics in Brussels. In the words of its final communiqué, the participants 'benefited from a high degree of convergence between people of different cultures, East and West, and a variety of disciplines'. There was absolute unanimity among those present that the main need of individuals and nations alike was to practise responsible stewardship. On behalf of the conference, I chaired a Working Party over the succeeding year to formulate a 'Code of Environmental Practice' (reprinted in Berry 1993b). The code went to the G7 Heads of State meeting in Texas in 1990. It is based on a simple ethic: *stewardship of the living and non-living systems of the earth in order to maintain their sustainability for present and future, allowing development with forbearance and fairness*. In itself, this is an innocuous statement, indeed almost vacuous. Acceptance of it, however, demands characteristics common to all good citizens, as well as states and corporations, involving responsibility, freedom, justice, truthfulness, sensitivity, awareness and integrity. In turn these lead to a series of obligations which are its teeth and may involve real cost.

The Code is a secular document, produced by a secular group for a secular organization. It was one of the documents submitted as a source paper for the 'Earth Charter' which was intended to preface the work of the UN Conference on Environment and Development in Rio (but which succumbed to political expediency, and was replaced by an anodyne 'Rio Declaration', Grubb *et al*. 1993). But it was taken almost in its entirety by a Working Party of the General Synod of the Church of England charged with preparing 'a statement of Christian stewardship in relation to the whole of creation to challenge government, Church and people' (*Christians and the Environment*, 1991). The General Synod paper began with a statement of Christian understanding:

> We all share and depend on the same world, with its finite and often non-renewable resources. Christians believe that this world belongs to God by

creation, redemption and sustenance and that he has entrusted it to humankind, made in his image and responsible to him; we are in the position of stewards, tenants, curators, trustees or guardians, whether or not we acknowledge this responsibility.

Stewardship implies caring management, not selfish exploitation; it involves a concern for both present and future as well as self, and a recognition that the world we manage has an interest in its own survival and wellbeing independent of its value to us.

It then drew out the implications of such stewardship in the same way (and in almost the same language) as the Brussels Code. Christian doctrine provides an additional theoretical underpinning for the secular conclusions, but the practical outworking of both sacred and secular is identical – as indeed Christians ought to expect, since they believe that God created, ordained and sustains the world for righteous and unrighteous alike. Orthodox Christian doctrine says that God is both transcendent and immanent: outside and controlling the world, and inside and influencing it (as anyone who prays in faith accepts). Leading British green, Jonathan Porritt, has claimed that the Christian error is to believe in a God far away and remote, whereas the discovery of green religionists is that God is within and intimate (Porritt & Winner 1988). Porritt's version demonstrates only too clearly the church's failure to claim and expound sound doctrine, as well as the greens' acceptance of a half-truth as potentially distorting, as was the opposite half-truth, exemplified two centuries ago by Paley's 'Divine Watchmaker'.

An important element in the Christian doctrine of the environment is the separation of God and creation. The clear teaching of the Bible is that the link between Creator and created is the Word of God; creation is not divine, it is not God, and it is related to God through us ('made in God's image'). The problem ought not to be walking a tightrope between immanence and transcendence, but an unapologetic trinitarianism; the world is redeemed from being merely an object by Christ's work, and is upheld and ordered by the Spirit. If we see the way forward as a balance between a distant God of absolute power and a confusing panentheism, we will find ourselves repeatedly having to readjust the balance. If, on the other hand, we follow Irenaeus and Tertullian in insisting on a God who alone is self-existent and who created out of nothing, we avoid the dangers of both dualism and a self-centred religion knowable only through self-realization. The contemporary New Age debate is really a rerun of the gnostic debate of the early centuries AD.

All this means that there is more to a Christian understanding of the environment than calculating stewardship. If we are not careful, stewardship becomes just one more command to obey; indeed in the industrial world, environmental care is commonly reduced to conformity in meeting statutory requirements, rather than an attitude of respect and moral responsibility. Chris Patten, when British Environment Minister, described the Christian idea well:

> The relationship between man and his environment depends, and always will depend, on more than just sound science and sound economics. For individuals part of the relationship is metaphysical. Those of us with religious convictions can, if we are lucky, experience the beauties as well as the utilities of the world as direct manifestations of the love and creative power of God.

Conclusions

A major part of the 'metaphysical relationship' extolled by Patten is experiential. It was awe and wonder which led such different characters as John Muir, Julian Huxley and Pierre Teilhard de Chardin to seek a rationalization for their experiences. It is more than a quest or challenge, or a desire for like-companionship, that produces escape to the wilds. But I would urge that there is something deeper, towards which wilderness-seekers are groping. Whether the symptoms are middle-class involvement in recycling, countryside protection or eco-consumerism, or more radical New Age commitments to self-discovery, there is a widespread recognition of a missing 'order' in modern society. This may be the reason for 'return to nature' cults; other people's grass is always greener than one's own, and native societies are commonly perceived to have a wisdom and peace that have disappeared from more advanced cultures. But this is an illusion (p. 106).

Moreover, we live in a fallen world, and this involves nature as well as ourselves. As Paul wrote, 'The creation was subjected to frustration . . . We know that the whole creation has been groaning as in the pains of childbirth right up to the present time' (Rom. 8:20, 22). This is often interpreted as a description of God's punishment to Adam and Eve, which introduced a range of biological and geological 'curses' such as weeds, pathogens and earthquakes. Unfortunately for such exegesis, the

Bible is singularly inexplicit about the effects of the fall, with the key exception that death entered the world through Adam's disobedience (Rom. 5:12; 1 Cor. 15:21–22). But as we have seen (p. 51), death in the Bible is not about disease and decay; principally it is about separation from God, and only secondarily about physical death. Paul's point is that as long as we refuse (or fail) to play the part assigned to us by God (that is, to act as his stewards or vicegerents here on earth), so long is the entire world of nature frustrated and dislocated; an untended garden is one which is overrun by thorns and thistles.

Charles Cranfield (1974) expresses this powerfully in expounding the Romans passage. He asks:

What sense can there be in saying that 'the sub-human creation – the Jungfrau, for example, or the Matterhorn, or the planet Venus – suffers frustration by being prevented from properly fulfilling the purpose of its existence?' The answer must surely be that the whole magnificent theatre of the universe, together with all its splendid properties and all the varied chorus of sub-human life, created for God's glory, is cheated of its true fulfilment so long as man, the chief actor in the great drama of God's praise, *fails to contribute his rational part*. The Jungfrau and the Matterhorn and the planet Venus and all living things too, man alone excepted, do indeed glorify God in their own ways; but, since their praise is destined to be not a collection of independent offerings but part of a magnificent whole, the united praise of the whole creation, they are prevented from being fully that which they were created to be, *so long as man's part is missing*, just as all the other players in a concerto would be frustrated of their purpose if the soloist were to fail to play his part [my italics].

An interesting complement to this is given by Robin Grove-White (1992). Building on the conclusion by Lynn White that 'what we do about ecology depends on our ideas of the man–nature relationship', Grove-White writes:

[It] has been largely unrecognized in recent theological discussion of the environmental crisis that the orthodox description of the phenomenon embodies a seriously inadequate conception of human nature at its very centre. Indeed . . . rather than the environmental agenda being presented to us from on high by science, the actual selection of issues . . . arises from human beings responding gropingly to a sense of the ways in which their moral, social and physical identities are being threatened.

He identifies the way forward as new theological understandings of the human person and its needs. I believe he is right in seeing the key to environmental sense in human nature; but we do not need *new* understandings; our starting-point is the ancient, universally established, and often disguised selfishness and pride of the individual. Our *greed* is at the root of all environmental damage – sometimes expressed as personal wants, sometimes through corporate action, sometimes as a simple desire to demonstrate power (Bratton 1992). This is ground common to all major religions. The distinguishing trait of the Christian faith is that God has taken action to deal with the problem (*e.g.* Col. 1:16–20). Christians have a particular responsibility to the environment because of their acknowledgment and worship of God as creator, redeemer and sustainer. For them, abuse of the natural world is disobedience to God, not merely an error of judgment. This means that Christians must examine their lifestyle and work out their attitude to the natural world as part of their service and stewardship. It also means affirming a God who is neither remote nor powerless. The Church of England Doctrine Commission put it thus:

> To accept God as the Creator of all things implies that man's own creative activity should be in co-operation with the purposes of the Creator who has made all things good. To accept man's sinfulness is to recognize the limitation of human goals and the uncertainty of human achievement. To accept God as Saviour is to work out our own salvation in union with him, and so to do our part in restoring and recreating what by our folly and frailty we have defaced or destroyed, and in helping to come to birth those good possibilities of creation that have not yet been realised . . . To hold that God has created the world for a purpose gives man a worthy goal in life and a hope to lift up his heart and to strengthen his efforts. To believe that man's true citizenship is in heaven and that his true identity lies beyond space and time enables him both to be involved in this world and yet to have a measure of detachment from it that permits radical changes such as would be scarcely possible if all his hopes were centred on this world. To believe that all things will be restored and nothing wasted gives added meaning to all man's efforts and strivings. Only by the inspiration of such a vision is society likely to be able to re-order this world and to find the symbols to interpret man's place within it (Montefiore 1975:77).

The tragedy of modern society – even that part which worships God – is that (in J. B. Phillips's words) its God is too small. The God of twentieth-century westerners is a God of the gaps, squeezed into the ever-shrinking gaps of knowledge. But the Christian God is Lord of all; he is Lord of creation as well as of the church. God so loved the *cosmos* – not merely the human world – that he sent his only Son to die for it.

The church has too often acquiesced with secular humanism in downgrading human beings as 'nothing but' animals, with the implication that we are only part of a large and intricate ecological machine (Barnett 1988). The challenge to the church from reason, tradition and Scripture is that we are stewards in God's world, accountable to him for our behaviour towards the whole of creation. The challenge *from* the church to the world is twofold. First, we all – individually and corporately – should be responsible managers of our environment; acceptance of this responsibility is a necessary preliminary to inheriting our privileges in this life. Secondly, God has a plan for each one of us, which involves repentance and reconciliation through Christ:

> For by him all things were created, things in heaven and on earth, visible and invisible, whether thrones or powers or rules or authorities . . . God was pleased to have all his fulness dwell in him, and through him to reconcile to himself all things, whether things on earth or things in heaven, by making peace through his blood, shed on the cross (Col. 1:16–20).

In the middle of the Acts of the Apostles are three verses which record Paul's only address to those outside mainstream religious thought. There are plenty of examples in the New Testament of sermons directed to educated Jews, to academics who suspect that there is a supernatural dimension, or to believers with incomplete understanding. How does Paul challenge postmodern men and women? You might think that he would take the opportunity to preach 'Christ and him crucified', or the incarnation, or resurrection, or reconciliation, or the warmth of church fellowship. He does none of these things. His message is simple: it is one of hope and of the good news of God at work; it is a straightforward plea to take the facts of human folly and the works of God in nature at their face value. Paul says:

> We are bringing you good news, telling you to turn from these worthless things to the living God, who made heaven and earth and sea and everything

in them. In the past, he let all nations go their own way. Yet he has not left himself without testimony: He has shown kindness by giving you rain from heaven and crops in their seasons; he provides you with plenty of food and fills your hearts with joy (Acts 14:15–17).

In a world in which we are increasingly having to question the regularity of the seasons or the trustworthiness of the rains, let us seize on the clue to God's nature that he has given us in the benefits we receive (Houghton 1994). Our world is not a chance collection of atoms, nor are we simply generalized higher apes. We live in a world created by God, and we are responsible to him for our treatment of it. Let us not apologize for the faith of our fathers. The God of Abraham, Elijah and David is the God of history, who is active today. Our ways are in his hands; he is the God of AD 2000 just as much as he was the God of 2000 BC or of AD 1000.

6

AFFIRMATION

Genesis 1:1, Yorkshire Dialect Translation

First on
There was silence.
And God said:
'Let there be clatter.'

The wind, unclenching,
Runs its thumbs
Along dry bristles of Yorkshire Fog.

The mountain ousel
Oboes its one note.

After rain
Water lobelia
Drips like a tap
On the tarn's tight surface-tension.

But louder,
And every second nearer,
Like chain explosions
From furthest nebulae
Light-yearning across space:
The thudding of my own blood.

'It's nobbut me,'
Says God.

Norman Nicholson (1914–87)
From *Sea to the West* (1981)

I have already quoted the words of Ecclesiastes, 'Of making many books there is no end, and much study wearies the body . . . Fear God and keep his commandments, for this is the whole duty of man' (12:12–13) (p. 57). When I was a student at university, I had this pinned above my bed. At that time of my life, this was the cynicism (or perhaps the desperation) of a young Christian required to master more and more facts and ideas. But the author (he calls himself 'the Preacher') was sounding a warning about being uncritical, not providing a let-out. Charles Spurgeon wrote of the need for hard labour: 'the would-be wise man will make his study a prison and his books the warders of a gaol.' Since the 1960s new religious movements have mushroomed. Sociologists may have delighted in describing our world as secular, but the evidence is that, having turned from mainline traditional religions, people have easily accepted a plethora of new religions, some of them manifestly absurd. Eastern cults, Transcendental Meditation, Jonestown, Scientology, the Children of God, the Moonies and a variety of other religious novelties claim to hold out answers to the very questions the Preacher has been facing and which traditional churches have failed to address.

The same is true of theories about Jesus. One moment someone has discovered that 'God is an astronaut', the next that he was the founder of a mushroom cult. Theories about Jesus zoom down upon us like reports of the latest marvels of computer technology. If you miss one exciting story, don't worry! There will be another one any minute.

The Preacher warns against going after intellectual dilettantism. His advice is to stick to the ancient and tried wisdom. Novelties appear attractive, but an honest mind examining them tends to find that not only do they have little going for them, but they are very deceptive in method and quite destructive in result. The evidence for such a conclusion in our own day abounds.

We must sadly confess that the failure of the church to present the authentic Christian message in a forthright and attractive way has often driven people to turn elsewhere. I believe that those of us who are both scientists and Christians must bear some of the blame for this, although we have been grievously hindered by Christians who talk nonsense about science, or about the significance of their interpretation of the Bible as it applies to the world around us. The tragedy is that we have not been forceful enough to insist that it is entirely reasonable to believe in a supernatural God who acts in the world and who holds it in being through both normal and abnormal (or miraculous) events.

Nor have we been definite enough in testifying that it is possible to find answers to questions about the meaning of life. One of the problems of being a scientist is that we grow addicted to research itself, in love with our own hard questions. An answer would spoil everything. C. S. Lewis in *The Great Divorce* (1946:40) captures the tone and temper of this attitude, at the stage when it has wholly possessed a man. In a scene on the borders of heaven, a lifelong 'searcher' is invited in. He is told:

'I can promise you . . . no scope for your talents: only forgiveness for having perverted them. No atmosphere of inquiry, for I will bring you to the land not of questions but of answers, and you shall see the face of God.'

'Ah, but we must all interpret those beautiful words in our own way! For me there is no such thing as a final answer. The free wind of inquiry must always continue to blow through the mind, must it not? . . .'

'. . . Listen!' said the White Spirit. 'Once you were a child. Once you knew what inquiry was for. There was a time when you asked questions because you wanted answers, and were glad when you had found them. Become that child again: even now.'

'Ah, but when I became a man I put away childish things.'

This is not the scientific method; it is pure intellectual debauchery. No argument, no appeal, will avail against this infinite elasticity. The encounter, already fruitless, ends with the gentle sophist's remembering an appointment, making his apologies, and hurrying off to his discussion group in hell.

If all I manage to do in this book is to encourage its readers to ask more questions I shall have failed dismally. Of course I have not dealt with all the questions in the area of science and faith (I have barely touched on what some will see as the really important problems, such as what happened at and immediately after the Big Bang, or what is the relationship between mind and matter (on which see D. Wilkinson 1993; Jeeves 1994); and I am well aware that I have not answered all the questions which can (and do) arise about the topics I have dealt with. The purpose of this book is to show that we must be open to new ideas and new interpretations of old truths (including Bible passages), and not to argue ever more detailed and watertight revisionisms about the nature of life or our treatment of the world. Any such approach is flawed because it presupposes a static and self-contained universe. That way is to follow

John Milton (1608–74), who interwove a tremendous amount of Renaissance speculation into *Paradise Lost* and tied himself (and his contemporaries) in knots. He wrote (Book VIII):

> . . . Heav'n is as the Book of God before thee set,
> Wherein to read his wondrous Works . . .
> . . . whether Heav'n move to Earth,
> Imports not, if thou reckon right, the rest
> From Man or Angel the Great Architect
> Did wisely to conceal, and not divulge
> His secrets . . .

and then went on to describe also the frenetic attempts of medieval astronomers to rescue Ptolemy's cosmology, as they

> . . . build, unbuild, contrive
> To save appearances, how gird the Sphear
> With Centric and Eccentric scribl'd ore
> Cycle and Epicycle, Orb in Orb.

Such is the way of dispute and polemic, but not of science. Unfortunately it befuddles everybody: two centuries after Milton, the American geologist Edward Hitchcock wrote (1851): 'The theologians, having so mixed up the ideas of Milton with those derived from inspiration . . . find it difficult to distinguish between them.' Indeed, the eighteenth century and the first half of the nineteenth were dominated by the use of science as a crutch to support the Christian faith, rather than a scalpel to dissect the natural world, following the assertion of John Locke in *The Reasonableness of Christianity* (1695) that 'revelation is natural reason enlarged by a new set of discoveries communicated by God immediately, which reason vouches the truth of, by God'. In other words, the Bible was seen as giving no more than a sort of close-up enlargement of things we might be able to perceive in other ways.

Such an approach contains the seeds of all kinds of confusion, yet it is still used; some of the problems and dubious inferences about the nature of biological and human life arise precisely because reason and revelation remain scrambled in much current debate (chapter 4). I have described some of the unravelling of this in earlier pages, and also some of the extravagances to which speculation on the environment has led when unshackled from both reason and revelation. Notwithstanding, the frontier between science and religion remains beset with conflict and dissension. There are at least three reasons for this.

The first is *the misreading of the Bible*. Galileo was condemned for propagating the idea that the Earth moved when the Bible apparently said it was fixed (p. 18), and Paul had to answer charges that he was wilfully misrepresenting the Old Testament (*e.g.* Rom. 3:4, 6, 9). In just the same way, the intellectual descendants of these complainers persist in treating the Genesis 1 creation narrative as if it referred to a literal week of seven twenty-four-hour days, 6,000 years ago (despite the inanity of thereby assuming that God took the seventh day off and had a rest (p. 44); and disingenuously add to the Bible by claiming that 'life' begins at conception and that all life is sacred (p. 77). We must be ruthless in examining our *interpretations* of the Scriptures. This does not mean questioning in any way the authority of the Bible, but it does mean that we must continually check our understanding of it by confirming the consistency of our interpretations with all relevant scriptural statements, in the light of the intentions of the original authors, and in conformity with our best reading of God's other 'book', the 'book of nature'.

The second reason for conflict at the interface of science and faith is *the misusing of history*. The Bible is explicit in distinguishing between Christians and non-Christians (between sheep and goats, between those who have gone through the narrow gate as opposed to the wide one, between those who 'accept' Christ and those who do not), but it is wholly illegitimate to extrapolate from this distinction to all the beliefs and actions of Christians. For example, some claim that it is impossible for a Christian to be an evolutionist (Morris 1980), or to deny that a fertilized human egg should be afforded the same protection as an adult human being (p. 73), or to discriminate between human beings and other animals (Singer, 1976, has invented a new sin of speciesism). Such invidious inferences have been encouraged by the common but outmoded assumption of an inevitable conflict between science and faith, building on the debate between Thomas Henry Huxley and Bishop Wilberforce which was actually about completely different issues (p. 37). We must beware of misusing history (Brooke 1991).

The third source of conflict is *fear of change*. We are nervous about the unknown, and anything which leads to change and increases uncertainty is viewed with suspicion. Bishop Wilberforce raged against Darwinism because it threatened his beliefs about the innate stability of authority in society and religion; creationism is strongest among sociological conservatives (Cole 1983); attitudes to prenatal life arouse strong emotions, but we must certainly face the possibility that current beliefs will have to change when embryological facts eventually meet theological dogma (Dworkin 1993; Dyson 1995). But our God repeatedly led his people into the unknown or unexpected, and has given us his Spirit to overcome our natural fears (Rom. 8:15; 2 Tim. 1:7). If we are confident in our faith, we should be prepared to accept the challenges of new knowledge and not pretend that it is either intrinsically incorrect or inevitably inspired by the devil.

I firmly believe that science and faith should complement each other. I therefore end with seven affirmations recapitulating and hence to some extent repeating points made in earlier pages. My hope is that they will encourage those who have got this far; their aim is to reinforce my contention that a balanced understanding of life requires the reading of the books of both nature and Scripture.

1. We live in a world which is in principle understandable

This is almost a truism, but it needs emphasizing, because if our world were not orderly and predictable, science would not be possible. The danger, of course, is that we then go on to assume that everything is in principle foreseeable, and that if we once knew the starting conditions, we could know all the future including our own fate. Modern developments of chaos theory should have disabused us of such an extensive determinism (Houghton 1988), but even if we do live in a strongly deterministic universe, there is still room for free will (and therefore responsibility) and for God to carry out his own purposes. We may be part of a massive geobiophysical machine, but that does not excuse a naïve view of causation. Purpose and divine control act at a different but complementary level to physical linkages. An understanding and acceptance of modern science does not – and cannot – prove anything about the existence and activity of God.[1] As has often been said, the belief that miracles do not occur is just as much an act of faith as the belief that they do occur.

[1] Any discussion of God's activity involves the question whether God uses 'natural means' to carry out his purposes. In this context, the attitude of Hudson Taylor (1832–1905), founder of the China Inland Mission (now the Overseas Missionary Fellowship), is relevant, particularly since he is often quoted as a man of extraordinary faith. On his first

2. God has revealed himself to us

God has revealed himself in his written Word, as well as in the Word made flesh, Jesus Christ. It surely makes sense that if there is a God, he will want to communicate with us, and the obvious and normal way to communicate is through words. Explicitly, I believe that the Bible is the major channel of communication to us from God. This faith is entirely independent of the mechanism by which God caused his words to be transmitted. Paul says that all Scripture (which meant for him the Old Testament) is 'God-breathed' (2 Tim. 3:16), perhaps a similar process to the way in which God's image was 'impressed' on the clay of the first truly human being (Gn. 2:7). This was not a simple matter of God using automata, but one which allowed the writers to make use of all their academic abilities (Lk. 1:1–14).

---

voyage to China, his ship ran into a fierce storm. Looking back, Hudson Taylor wrote: 'One thing was a great trouble to me that night. I was a very young believer, and had not sufficient faith in God to see Him in and through the use of means. I had felt it a duty to comply with the earnest wish of my beloved and honoured mother, and for her sake to procure a swimming-belt. But in my own soul I felt as if I could not simply trust in God while I had this swimming-belt, and my heart had no rest until on that night, after all hope of being saved was gone, I had given it away.

'Ever since, I have seen clearly the mistake I made; a mistake that is very common in these days, when erroneous teaching on faith-healing does much harm, misleading some as to the purposes of God, shaking the faith of others and distressing the minds of many. The use of means ought not to lessen our faith in God, and our faith in God ought not to hinder our using whatever means He has given us for the accomplishment of His own purposes.

'For years after this I always took a swimming-belt with me and never had any trouble about it; for after the storm was over, the question was settled for me through the prayerful study of the Scriptures. God gave me then to see my mistake, probably to deliver me from a great deal of trouble on similar questions now so constantly raised. When in medical or surgical charge of any case, I have never thought of neglecting to ask God's guidance and blessing in the use of appropriate means, nor yet of omitting to give thanks for answered prayer and restored health. But to me it would appear as presumptuous and wrong to neglect the use of those measures which He Himself has put within our reach, as to neglect to take daily food and suppose that life and health might be maintained by prayer alone.' (Quoted from Hudson Taylor's *Retrospect* in Dr and Mrs Howard Taylor, *Hudson Taylor in Early Years*, 1: *The Growth of the Soul*, p. 191. London: CIM, 1911.)

In fact the inspiration and authority of the Bible are secondary to those of Jesus Christ. *If* Jesus was truly God as he claimed (*e.g.* Jn. 14:10–11; *cf.* Heb. 1:3), and *if* his death was a triumph over death (Mk. 15:37–39; 1 Pet. 3:18; *etc.*) by which our separation and alienation from God can be overcome (Acts 4:12; Heb. 10:14), then the records of him achieve a special significance (*e.g.* Jn. 1:1–14) and the Old Testament has to be interpreted in terms of the accounts and implications of Christ's life, death and claims in the New Testament. All discussion about the accuracy or inerrancy of the Bible is subsidiary to this. We have to begin from the historically well-attested accounts of Christ and decide whether he was who he claimed to be, because if he was not, he was a paranoid megalomaniac. There is no valid option of regarding Jesus as merely a great teacher and example: he was either divine or deluded; and if he was divine, his death was an active victory over evil, not a disaster. In traditional theological language, the crucifixion and resurrection provide substitutionary atonement, making it possible for us to be justified by faith (Rom. 3:22–24; 5:1–2).

Such language and ideas are not foreign to a scientist, because they begin with the evidence we have (Jesus Christ and his nature) and then explore the consequences of accepting the evidence. Any honest person should go from this to check the coherence of the Christian gospel and see if it stands up to any tests that we make. The tests are consistency and subjective experience (that is, God's transforming grace and answers to prayer). This is exactly the logic that was presented to me after my father's suicide and my own search for meaning in life (p. 4). In fact, it brings us right back to George Porter's statement that 'there is one great purpose for us today, and that is to try to discover man's purpose by every means in our power' (p. 29). It is possible to do this, but we will not be successful unless we use all the evidence available to us; that is, unless we read the books of both Scripture and nature. Otherwise we will be like people trying to find our way by admiring the scenery but not bothering with the map.

3. We live in God's world, and we are his stewards

By faith, the Christian believes that God created the world (Gn. 1:1; Heb. 11:3); by reason, we learn something of the timings and methods through which the world as we know it has come about. In other words, there is a credible scientific account of chemical, geological and biological evolution which complements the religious account. The Bible tells us something of the meaning of the world in which we live (that is, it deals with 'Why?' questions); science deals with the mechanisms by which evolution occurred, which are not described in the Bible (that is, science answers 'How?' questions).

But Christians go further: they believe that this is God's world by creation (Pss. 24:1; 104:5–6) and redemption (Jn. 3:16), and because he sustains it (Ps. 104:27–30; Col. 1:17; Heb. 1:13); and that it is intrinsically good (Gn. 1:31; Ps. 19:1; 1 Tim. 4:4). And one stage even further still is that God has entrusted this creation to us, to be his stewards, tenants, curators, trustees or guardians, whether or not we acknowledge this responsibility (Hall 1986). Adam and Eve were placed in a garden to tend it; plants and animals are for us to eat (Gn. 9:3) as well as to look after for God. Conservation, not preservation, is the Christian mandate.

Matthew Fox has rejected 'the stewardship model (that God is an absentee landlord and we humans are serfs, running the garden for God); it does not appeal to the young or to our hearts – it is just one more duty, one more commandment to follow . . . We need mysticism – God IS the garden' (lecture given at St James' Church, Piccadilly, London). This is an heterodox and unscriptural rejection of stewardship. A more cogent criticism is that of Mary Jegen (1987):

> Stewardship has failed where it has been reduced to a reasonable way of managing time, talent and treasure for the sake of the kingdom as we understand it; where it has not created a moral and religious imperative for rectifying the massive structural injustices that make life short and cruel for millions; where it has not moved people to commit themselves to changing the structures that support injustice.

As we have seen, our Lord's teaching is full of examples and exhortations to accept responsibility for our actions in all spheres of life. For example, we are told about the wicked husbandmen who were not content to manage sustainably the vineyard entrusted to them, but took all the renewable resources for themselves, and attempted to expropriate the capital as well (Lk. 20:9–19). Because of their failure of stewardship, they were punished severely by the owner of the vineyard when he returned to find out what was going on. In the context, this is primarily a parable of the way the Israelites would kill God's Son, but it speaks also of their task of straightforward environmental management; their poor stewardship was firmly and massively judged.

In the gospels of Mark and Luke, this parable is preceded and followed by teaching about Christ's own authority; in Matthew's gospel, another parable about obedience over environmental work is put between the questioning about Jesus' authority and the parable of the wicked husbandmen, and it is followed by the parable of the wedding banquet, which is also about judgment (Mt. 21:23 – 22:21). We have been given a job to do, and it matters how we do it.

4. We are animals, but we are in God's image

One of the most brutally realistic books about religion is Bertrand Russell's *Why I Am Not a Christian*. It is realistic because it faces up to the emptiness of being 'merely' an animal, much more so than, for example, Jacques Monod's *Chance and Necessity*. But one of the oddities of Russell's approach is that he lauds Science, for which he consistently uses a capital 'S'; he effectively deifies it.

Almost as bad is the attitude in some Christian writing that there is an invariant sober and sombre Christian 'type' which should be the goal of all those whom God has called. This is not the Bible description of a Christian. God has called some to be prophets and some teachers; to some he has given gifts of healing, to some gifts of administration, and so on; some are here to do public jobs, some the less presentable ones. The point is that we all have talents and we are expected to use them (Mt. 25:14–30; 13:3–23), however difficult the conditions (Mt. 13:24–30). If we do not, we shall be judged, just as the bad stewards were.

But we are not just left alone to try hard. In the first place we have God's image, which has been marred by the rebellion which we call the fall, but is still there in each one of us. And secondly, those of us who are Christians have God's Spirit in us and the confidence that 'in all things God works for the good of those who love him, who have been called according to his purpose. For those God foreknew he also predestined to be conformed to the likeness of his Son . . . in all things we are more than conquerors through him who loved us' (Rom. 8:28–29, 37).

5. God is both transcendent and immanent

God is the divine Creator who made all things and is seated in heaven, but he is also the one at work within us upholding everyday events and answering the prayers of his faithful people (Jn. 16:24). The God of the eighteenth century was a 'Great Watchmaker' who had made all things well, but then retired above the bright blue sky, remote from normal life and problems. There is a considerable irony in the fact that it was the Darwinian revolution that removed the necessity for the 'Great Watchmaker', the first cause, and as a result brought God back into the world he had made, as upholder and sustainer as well as creator (p. 55).

The relationship of God to the world, and to us and our lives, is perhaps the most important question there is. It is the question which science is popularly supposed to have dealt with by removing God from the world, but which, as we have seen, has done no such thing. It is the responsibility and the particular contribution of scientists who are Christians to explain how God can be active in processes for which we have another explanation; to explode, in other words, the insidious fallacy of 'nothing buttery' (p. 20). We have seen that we can properly and logically think of events having both a mechanical and a final cause (p. 22), and that there is no conflict in being able to give a full and satisfying 'scientific' description of some event and at the same time accepting a complementary explanation of the same physical happening. Because of its methodology, science has not excluded and cannot exclude God from being a necessary cause of any event.

This understanding of complementary explanation is crucial to recognizing that God can be accepted by 'thinking men and women' in a scientific or postmodern age or whatever we want to call it. Its neglect produces recurring frustrations and crises of belief. For example, in his book *Miracles*, C. S. Lewis (1947) defined a miracle as 'an interference with Nature by supernatural power' (p. 15); Nature is 'what happens "of itself" or "of its own accord"' (p. 16). This implies that Nature (Lewis uses a capital 'N') is a cosmic power, an idea which comes from Greek philosophy, not from the Bible. Lewis calls again on the Greeks (especially Plato) when he speaks of 'an eternal self-existent Reason' (capital 'R') which 'must exist and must be the source of my own imperfect and intermittent rationality' (p. 36). He was forced to believe like this because he was persuaded by J. B. S. Haldane's argument that 'if my mental processes are determined wholly by the motions of atoms in my brain, I have no reason for supposing my beliefs are true'. This is the flaw: Lewis accepted the common assumption that we cannot escape from a massive causal network, which in his case he attributed to an external 'Reason' in order to free himself from physical events in the brain. But this smacks of medieval astronomers flailing around to rescue Ptolemy's understanding of the universe. Lewis fell into the fallacy of 'nothing buttery' (p. 22) by assuming that the causal linkages of nerve connections rule out the possibility of free will and divine action. In fact it does no such thing, as we have seen: a physicist's explanation of the working of a computer in terms of the flow of electrons need not undermine a mathematician's explanation in terms of the calculation he has programmed it to perform.[2]

True science and truth faith should produce complementary interpretations of any phenomenon. If there is conflict, the proper step is to examine both explanations to test whether they are reasonable interpretations of the data. It is *not* correct simply to assume that one or the other must be wrong (for example, that a universal flood once so disrupted geological strata that it is completely impossible to make any sense of the fossil record; or conversely, that the close genetic relationship of the apes to *Homo sapiens* means that the Bible account of creation, Adam and Eve, the fall and so on is a pure fairy tale).

6. The Christian faith does not explain evil, but provides a solution for its effects

A conventional believer has to accept that there are many things he or she cannot understand. There is no shame in this, just as an honest scientist accepts that there are questions about meaning and purpose which

---

[2]This criticism of C. S. Lewis's interpretation of miracles is based on an article by Stuart Judge (1991), who refers to the working out of the complementary-explanation position in two books by Donald MacKay: chapter 4 of *The Clockwork Image* (1974) and chapter 2 of *Human Science and Human Dignity* (1979). A very similar position is developed by the psychologist Malcolm Jeeves (1984), who also acknowledges his debt to MacKay. It is relevant to record that Roger Penrose (1989) is another who has argued in this way, without any religious presuppositions or intentions. Penrose maintains that conscious awareness is a property of our brains, but it is something wholly different from computational-type thinking. His starting-point is the theorem proposed by Kurt Gödel in 1931, that any formal mathematical system of rules will be necessarily incomplete because there will always be truths outside the rules. It takes a vision of the system to create the system of rules, and that vision is never encompassed by the rules themselves. Penrose points out that this is a fair description of the relationship between a computer, its programme (system of rules), and its programmer (us). The computer itself can never get outside its own programme, but we can. Penrose's thesis has attracted considerable criticisms, to which he has replied at length (Penrose 1994).

science cannot and never will be able to answer (p. 22). The significant point for the believer is that there is a 'way' to overcome evil and wrong; the unique feature of the Christian faith is that God himself has prepared the way and made it attainable (Jn. 14:6; Acts 4:12).

This is not the place to enter into a discussion about evil, but one point is worth repeating in the context of the interface of science and faith: God is distinct and independent of his creation; he does not need it, nor is it a necessary corollary of his existence (pp. 39, 47, 102). This means that nature is not God (pantheism) nor is God contained in nature (as well as being beyond and outside it) (panentheism). Christians have always eschewed pantheism (cf. Is. 44:14–18; Jn. 1:1–3; Col. 1:16–20), although Teilhard de Chardin seems to have believed in something close to it with his notion of all creation coming together in fulfilment with the glorified Christ at the 'Omega Point'. His ideas have been roundly criticized (e.g. Jones 1969); suffice it here to say that they are not based on Scripture; they depend on a scientific and theological orthogenesis for which there is no evidence, and, although avowedly Christocentric, contain hope but no gospel. Panentheism, on the other hand, has a wide following in some theological circles, because it provides a way of envisaging God's immanence without denying his transcendence. It has been nourished by the process theologians (especially Charles Hartshorne and John Cobb); their ideas have links to liberation theology and have been particularly influential in World Council of Churches pronounce-ments. This theology has developed from a conviction that God cannot be impassive to suffering in the world; as he is affected by it, he responds and therefore changes through time. Closer examination, however, shows the difficulty of the concept. As Christian theology it is seriously defective because it relegates Christ's death to that of a mere catalyst within history, and empties it of all eternal significance.

True Christian affirmation is of a God who is infinite and changeless, who is outside time and therefore knows the future as well as the past, and, having given us free will and (and, some would say, thereby consciously limited himself), allows us to make or mar our lives. But – and this is a major qualification – he has actively intervened through Christ's coming to earth and dying for us, so that there is a way out of the morass in which we flounder as we exercise our freedom.

7. God has a purpose

God has not merely created the world and thrown it into space (that God is akin to Paley's Divine Watchmaker), but put us here to glorify him and to enjoy him for ever. To the unbeliever, this is empty arrogance; to the believer it is a purpose for living (pp. 55–56).

We can discern purpose at three levels. First, as animals, we are commanded 'to be fruitful and increase in number' (Gn. 1:22, 28), living as members of an interdependent and sustainable society (Dt. 20:19–20; 1 Cor. 11:11–12; 12:27). But we are not *mere* animals; we are transformed by 'God's image'. For example, the command to multiply was given without qualification; in ancient Israel children were regarded as a gift from God, and a couple gained a kind of immortality through their children. Once Christ came, the situation changed: life is 'brought to light by the appearing of our Saviour Jesus Christ' (2 Tim. 1:10). No other form of immortality remains relevant. The Old Testament commands about procreation (or non-contraception) have an explicit cut-off point in Christ.

This helps us to look at the other commands given in the first chapters of Genesis (they are often called 'creation ordinances') (Murray 1957). We clearly ought to interpret them in the context in which they were given, which relates to God's revelation of his own nature. We are never authorized to act towards his creation (either inanimate or animate) in ways or from motives which are foreign to that nature. If we regard the Ten Commandments as formal descriptions of our nature given to enable us to function more efficiently, we are more likely to obey them intelligently than if we take them as mere restrictions imposed by a distant God. One of the New Testament Greek words for salvation, *sōtēria*, means 'wholeness' or 'health'.

The command of God to refrain from eating 'of the tree of the knowledge of good and evil' (Gn. 2:17) is of another category. This injunction seems to be entirely arbitrary, if not petty; it is obviously different from the other ordinances – and because of the consequences of disobeying it, highly significant. If, however, the creation ordinances can be taken as describing 'properties' of humans (just as a car handbook lists laws framed in terms of the 'properties' of the car), this command becomes a description of our dependence upon God, a dependence which requires obedience. We have already seen that it is difficult to distinguish qualitatively between animals and humans (p. 48), but that the distinguishing factor seems to be one that involves obedience (pp. 53, 76). This is an unfashionable doctrine and science *cannot* provide a causal basis for it. This does not prove that it is unnecessary.

An analogy with drug dependence may help: drug addicts can have their addiction 'transferred' to other drugs, foods, their doctors, even religion – but they remain physiologically and psychologically dependent on something or somebody. In precisely the same way, we are spiritually 'designed' for dependence on God and we ignore or avoid this dependence at our peril. This is expressed in a formal way in the first three of the Ten Commandments, or in Christ's words, 'Love the Lord your God with all your heart and with all your soul and with all your mind and with all your strength' (Mk. 12:30).

Health has been described as 'the strength to be human'. True health, as distinct from the absence of disease, involves living in the truly human niche – and God is the basic provider of that niche (Fergusson 1993).

Secondly, as unique individuals, each with talents and failings, we have to discover our own role in life. God has a role for each one of us (Eph. 2:10; Phil. 3:15); the problem is to find it, and not merely follow the crowd. The story of Peter's dream in Acts 10:9–20 is instructive here: Peter was told in his dream to eat 'unclean animals', something which his whole background and education condemned. He took a lot of convincing, but eventually his prejudices were broken down, and he began to mix with non-Jews and played a key role in the transformation of the infant church from Jewish sect to worldwide mission. We can complain that Peter was not treated in the same way as we, and that we cannot rely on visions or voices from the Lord, but the message is clear: we need to examine preconceptions and knee-jerk responses and seek by prayer, advice and ruthless common sense to find God's will for ourselves.

Moreover, we need to be alert for differences in his will for us from one phase of our life to another. Too many people assume that the place or job that God has for them when young will remain unchanging. We need to be continually aware that he may have new challenges or opportunities for us – particularly when we least expect them.

Finally, we are part of God's overall purpose, working towards the time when he will come again. We do not know when this will be (and Christ himself advised us not to put energy or hope into trying to find out). All that is certain is that at the end there will be two groups, those whose names are 'written in the Lamb's book of life' and those whose names are not so written. Therein lies the urgency of response to the gospel of salvation.

This moves us far from the subject matter of this book into the realm of pure religion. I will abstain from developing this theme: my aim in these pages is far more modest; it is to point to the way that proper faith and proper science fit together and to urge that they be studied in partnership rather than in isolation or, worse, in opposition.

The wisdom writings of the Old Testament repeatedly warn that 'the fear of the LORD is the beginning of wisdom'. Psalm 111 concludes with this phrase, qualifying the ever-present danger of worshipping the creation by pointing us to the Creator. And that is where our ambition should be. We need a mature doctrine of creation, not the emasculated one of the 'creationists' who fail to read properly the books of nature; not the empty one of the liberals who censor the books of nature and Scripture so severely that it is difficult to find where God is; not the mutilated one of the deists, who push God so far away that he becomes irrelevant; not the sacramental one of the panentheists and their allies, who seek to fit God to their own perceptions; and not the God of the philosophers who has to be small enough to fit into the gaps of their understanding. Only when we are bold and brave enough to face up to the real world and to God's Word, written and made flesh, will we begin to have such a mature doctrine. Only then will we be able to develop a positive ethic of life and rightly discern the limits of humankind, and only then will we become good stewards of our own life and our environment.

It is fashionable to seek wisdom from primitive religion and native people. The danger is that we accept uncritically all they have to tell us; there is no necessary reason why their ways should be any purer than ours. But it is certainly worth peeling away the irrelevant shells in which we hide (De Waal 1991). We live in God's world; let us study and rejoice in that world: 'The heavens declare the glory of God; the skies proclaim the work of his hands' (Ps. 19:1).

Those of us who live in great cities and shield ourselves from the raw environment would do well to remember God's questions to Job (McKibben 1994):

> Who is this that darkens my counsel
>   with words without knowledge?
> Brace yourself like a man;
>   I will question you,

and you shall answer me.

Where were you when I laid the earth's foundation?
Tell me, if you understand.
Who marked off its dimensions? Surely you know!
Who stretched a measuring line across it?
On what were its footings set,
or who laid its cornerstone –
while the morning stars sang together
and all the angels shouted for joy?

(Jb. 38:2–7)

It is to be hoped that this will lead us to a humility in which we can share the contentment of Robert Rendall's Orkney crofter:

Scant are the few green acres I till,
But arched above them spreads the boundless sky,
Ripening their crops; and round them lie
Long miles of moorland hill.

Beyond the cliff-top glimmers in the sun
The far horizon's bright infinity;
And I can gaze across the sea
When my day's work is done.

The solitudes of land and sea assuage
My quenchless thirst for freedom unconfined
With independent heart and mind
Hold I my heritage.

(From *Country Sonnets*, 1946)

But the fact that we must hold on to above all, whatever our sophistication or education or cleverness, is the One described in the poem at the head of this chapter, 'nobbut God'. Our need is not great faith; it is faith in a great God.

FURTHER READING

When I was a student in the 1950s there were few helpful books on issues of science and faith. In those far-off days, the most-read books were Arthur Rendle Short's *Modern Discovery and the Bible* (1942) and the various works of Robert Clark (1949, 1960 and others), none of them particularly satisfying to someone with questions, but indicators that these issues were actually on the Christian agenda. Then Bernard Ramm produced *The Christian View of Science and Scripture* (1954), which was much more constructive. Since that time there has been a flood of books, good, bad and indifferent. It would be impracticable to list even a selection, because some would not be to everyone's taste, and too much would be read into the books not mentioned, although it would be improper to omit Ian Barbour's seminal *Issues in Science and Religion* (1966). I have expanded the Bibliography beyond the basic requirements by including a number of reviews and source works which I hope may be useful. It is worth noting that it contains a number of recent books by scientists who take a conservative view of the Bible, yet adopt a positive view of the interaction between science and a biblical faith. To those referred to in the text I add Henry (1978), R. T. Wright (1989), Forster & Marston (1989) and Poole (1992). The American Scientific Affiliation (Ipswich, MA) produces *Contemporary Issues in Science and Faith: An Annotated Bibliography* (3rd edn 1992) and, for readers wanting to dig deeper and wider than this book, it is probably best to refer to that.

BIBLIOGRAPHY

Ashby, E. (1975), *A Second Look at Doom*. Twenty-first Fawley Foundation Lecture. Southampton: University of Southampton.

————(1978), *Reconciling Man with the Environment*. London: Oxford University Press.

————(1993), Foreword. *Environmental Dilemmas*: xiv–xxii. Berry, R. J. (ed.). London: Chapman & Hall.

Ashby, E. & Andersòn, M. (1981), *The Politics of Clean Air*. Oxford: Clarendon.

Assisi Declarations: Messages on Man and Nature (1986). Gland, Switzerland: Worldwide Fund for Nature.

Attfield, R. (1983), *The Ethics of Environmental Concern*. Oxford: Basil Blackwell (revised edition 1991, Athens, GA: University of Georgia Press).

Austin, R. C. (1987), *Baptized into Wilderness: A Christian Perspective on John Muir*. Atlanta: John Knox.

Ayala, F. J. (1974), Introduction. *Studies in the Philosophy of Biology: Reductionism and Related Problems*: vii–xvi. Ayala, F. J. & Dobzhansky, Th. (eds.). London: Macmillan.

Barbour, I. G. (1966), *Issues in Science and Religion*. New York: Prentice-Hall.

Barnett, S. A. (1988), *Biology and Freedom*. Cambridge: Cambridge University Press.

Berry, A. C. (1987), *The Rites of Life*. London: Hodder & Stoughton.

————(1993), *Beginnings: Christian Views of the Early Embryo*. London: Christian Medical Fellowship.

Berry, R. J. (1975), *Adam and the Ape*. London: Falcon.

——————(1977, reprinted 1990), *Inheritance and Natural History*. London: Collins.

——————(1982), *Neo-Darwinism*. London: Edward Arnold.

——————(1987), 'The Theology of DNA'. *Anvil* 4:39–49.

——————(1986), 'What to Believe about Miracles'. *Nature* 322:321–322.

——————(1988), *God and Evolution*. London: Hodder & Stoughton.

——————(1989), 'Ecology: Where Genes and Geography Meet'. *Journal of Animal Ecology* 58:733–759.

——————(ed.) (1991), *Real Science, Real Faith*. Eastbourne: Monarch.

——————(1993a), 'Green Religion and Green Science'. *Journal of the Royal Society of Arts* 141:305–318.

——————(1993b), 'Environmental Concern'. In *Environmental Dilemmas*: 242–264. Berry, R. J. (ed.). London: Chapman & Hall.

——————(1995), 'Creation and the Environment'. *Science and Christian Belief* 7:21–43.

——————(1996), 'The Virgin Birth of Christ'. *Science and Christian Belief* 8:101–110.

Berry, R. J. & Bradshaw, A. D. (1992), 'Genes in the Real World'. In *Genes in Ecology*: 431–449. Berry, R. J., Crawford, T. J. & Hewitt, G. M. (eds.). Oxford: Blackwell Scientific Publications.

Birch, L. C., Eakin, W. & MacDaniel, J. B. (eds.) (1990), *Liberating Life. Contemporary Approaches to Ecological Theology*. Maryknoll, NY: Orbis.

Blocher, H. (1983), *In the Beginning*. Leicester: Inter-Varsity Press.

Bratton, S. P. (1983), 'The Ecotheology of James Watt'. *Environmental Ethics* 5:225–236.

——————(1992), 'Loving Nature: Eros or Agape?' *Environmental Ethics* 14:3–25.

Brearley, M. (1992), 'Matthew Fox and the Cosmic Christ'. *Anvil* 9:39–54.

Brennan, A. (1988), *Thinking about Nature*. Athens, GA: University of Georgia Press.

Brenton, T. (1994), *The Greening of Machiavelli*. London: Earthscan, for the Royal Institute of Environmental Affairs.

Brooke, J. H. (1991), *Science and Religion: Some Historical Perspectives*. Cambridge: Cambridge University Press.

Brunner, E. (1939), *Man in Revolt*. Guildford: Lutterworth.

Bryant, J. (1992), 'Mapping the Human Genome: The Human Genome Project'. *Science and Christian Belief* 4:105–125.

Caring for the Earth: A Strategy for Sustainable Living (1991). Gland, Switzerland: International Union for the Conservation of Nature, United Nations Environmental Programme, Worldwide Fund for Nature.

Carson, R. (1962), *Silent Spring*. Boston: Houghton Mifflin.

Christians and the Environment (1991). A Report by the Board for Social Responsibility. London: General Synod Miscellaneous Paper no. 367.

Clarke, R. E. D. (1949), *The Universe: Plan or Accident?* London: Paternoster.

————— (1960), *Christian Belief and Science: A Reconciliation and a Partnership*. London: English Universities Press.

Coghlan, M. J. (1990), *The Vatican, the Law, and the Human Embryo*. Basingstoke: Macmillan.

Cole, J. R. (1983), 'Scopes and Beyond: Antievolutionism and American Culture'. In *Scientists Confront Creationism*: 13–32. Godfrey, L. R. (ed.). New York: W. W. Norton.

Conservation and Development Programme for the UK (1983). A response to the World Conservation Strategy. London: Kogan Page.

Cranfield, C. E. B. (1974), 'Some Observations on Romans 8:19–21'. In *Reconciliation and Hope: New Testament Essays on Atonement and Eschatology presented to L. L. Morris on his 60th birthday*: 224–230. Banks, R. (ed.). Grand Rapids, MI: Eerdmans.

De Beer, G. R. (1940), *Embryos and Ancestors*. Oxford: Clarendon.

Desmond, A. (1994), *Huxley: The Devil's Disciple*. London: Michael Joseph.

Desmond, A. & Moore, J. R. (1991), *Darwin*. London: Michael Joseph.

De Waal, E. (1984), *Seeking God: The Way of St Benedict*. London: Collins.

————— (1991), *A World Made Whole: Rediscovering the Celtic Tradition*. London: HarperCollins.

De Witt, C. B. (ed.) (1991), *The Environment and the Christian. What Can We Learn from the New Testament?* Grand Rapids, MI: Baker.

Diamond, J. (1991), *The Rise and Fall of the Third Chimpanzee*. London: Vintage.

Draper, J. W. (1875), *History of the Conflict between Religion and Science*. London: International Scientific Series.

Duke of Edinburgh & Mann, M. (1989), *Survival or Extinction*. Windsor: St George's House.

Dunstan, G. R. (1984), 'The Moral Status of the Human Embryo: A Tradition Recalled'. *Journal of Medical Ethics* 10:38–44.

Dworkin, R. (1993), *Life's Dominion: An Argument about Abortion and Euthanasia*. New York: Alfred Knopf.

Dyson, A. (1995), *The Ethics of IVF*. London: Mowbray.

Edge, D. O. (ed.) (1964), *Experiment*. London: BBC Publications.

Edwards, R. G. (1983), The Horizon Lecture. 'Test-tube Babies: The Ethical Debate'. *The Listener*, 27 October.

Elsdon, R. (1992), *Greenhouse Theology*. Tunbridge Wells: Monarch.

Engel, J. R. (1993), 'The Role of Ethics, Culture and Religion in Conserving Biodiversity: A Blueprint for Research and Action'. In *Ethics, Religion and Biodiversity: Relations between Conservation and Cultural Values*: 183–214. Hamilton, L. S. (ed.). Cambridge: White Horse.

Faricy, R. (1982), *Wind and Sea Obey Him*. London: SCM.

Fergusson, A. (ed.) (1993), *Health: The Strength to be Human*. Leicester: Inter-Varsity Press.

Ford, N. M. (1988), *When Did I Begin?* Cambridge: Cambridge University Press.

Forster, R. & Marston, P. (1989), *Reason and Faith: Do Modern Science and Christian Faith Really Conflict?* Eastbourne: Monarch.

Fox, M. (1983), *Original Blessing: A Primer in Creation Spirituality*. Santa Fe, New Mexico: Bear & Co.

Futuyma, D. J. (1983), *Science on Trial*. New York: Pantheon.

Galton, F. (1869), *Hereditary Genius*. London: Macmillan.

Godfrey, L. R. (ed.) (1983), *Scientists Confront Creationism*. New York: W. W. Norton.

Golley, F. B. (1993), *A History of the Ecosystem Concept in Ecology*. New Haven: Yale University Press.

Golombok, S., Cook, R., Bish, A. & Murray, C. (1995), 'Families Created by the New Reproductive Technologies: Quality of Parenting and Social and Emotional Development of the Children'. *Child Development* 66:285–298.

Gould, S. J. (1981), *The Mis-Measure of Man*. New York: W. W. Norton.

Granberg-Michaelson, W. (ed.) (1987), *Tending the Garden*. Grand Rapids, MI: Eerdmans.

Grove-White, R. (1992), 'Human Identity and the Environment Crisis'. In *The Earth Beneath*: 13–34. Ball, J., Goodall, M., Palmer, C. & Reader, J. (eds.). London: SPCK.

Grubb, M., Koch, M., Thomson, K., Munson, A. & Sullivan, F. (1993), *The Earth Summit Agreements*. London: Earthscan, for the Royal Institute for International Affairs.

Gunning, J. & English, V. (1993), *Human* In Vitro *Fertilization: A Case Study in the Regulation of Medical Innovation*. Aldershot: Dartmouth.

Haldane, J. B. S. (1932), *The Causes of Evolution*. London: Longmans, Green.

Hall, D. J. (1986), *Imaging God: Dominion as Stewardship*. Grand Rapids, MI: Eerdmans.

Hamilton, W. D. (1964), 'The Genetical Evolution of Social Behaviour'. *Journal of Theoretical Biology* 7:1–52.

Helm, P. (ed.) (1987), *Objective Knowledge: A Christian Perspective*. Leicester: Inter-Varsity Press.

Henry, C. F. H. (ed.) (1978), *Horizons of Science: Christian Scholars Speak Out*. San Francisco: Harper & Row.

Hobhouse, L. T. (1913), *Development and Purpose: An Essay Towards a Philosophy of Evolution*. London: Macmillan.

Hoekema, A. A. (1986), *Created in God's Image*. Grand Rapids, MI: Eerdmans.

Holder, R. D. (1993), *Nothing but Atoms and Molecules?* Tunbridge Wells: Monarch.

Houghton, J. (1988), *Does God Play Dice?* Leicester: Inter-Varsity Press.

——————(1994), *Global Warming: An Investigation of the Evidence, the Implications and the Way Forward*. Oxford: Lion.

Hummel, C. E. (1986), *The Galileo Connection: Resolving Conflicts between Science and the Bible*. Downers Grove, IL: InterVarsity Press.

Huxley, A. (1932), *Brave New World*. London: Chatto & Windus.

Jacoby, A. (1968), *Señor Kon-Tiki*. London: Allen & Unwin.

Jeeves, M. A. (1984), *Behavioural Sciences: A Christian Perspective*. Leicester: Inter-Varsity Press.

——————(1994), *Mind Fields: Reflections on the Science of Mind and Brain*. Leicester: Apollos.

Jegen, M. E. (1987), 'The Church's Role in Healing the Earth'. In *Tending the Garden*: 93–113. Granberg-Michaelson, W. (ed.). Grand Rapids, MI: Eerdmans.

Jenkins, D. E. (1987), *God, Miracle and the Church of England*. London: SCM.

Jones, D. G. (1969), *Teilhard de Chardin: An Analysis and Assessment*. London: Tyndale.

——————(1991), 'Non-existence and its Relevance for Medical Ethics and Genetic Technology'. *Perspectives on Science and Faith* 43:75–81.

———————— (1994), 'The Human Embryo: Between Oblivion and Meaningful Life'. *Science and Christian Belief* 6:3–19.

Judge, S. (1991), 'How Not to Think about Miracles'. *Science and Christian Belief* 3:97–102.

Kevles, D. J. (1985), *In the Name of Eugenics*. New York: Alfred Knopf.

Kidner, D. (1967), *Genesis*. London: Tyndale.

Kitcher, P. (1982), *Abusing Science: The Case against Creationism*. Boston, MA: MIT Press.

Kruskal, W. (1988), 'Miracles and Statistics: The Casual Assumption of Independence'. *Journal of the American Statistical Association* 83:929–940.

Leopold, A. (1949), *A Sand County Almanac*. New York: Oxford University Press.

Lewis, C. S. (1946), *The Great Divorce*. London: Geoffrey Bles.

———————— (1947), *Miracles*. London: Geoffrey Bles.

———————— (1962), *The Problem of Pain*. London: Geoffrey Bles.

Livingstone, D. N. (1987), *Darwin's Forgotten Defenders: The Encounter Between Evangelical Theology and Evolutionary Thought*. Grand Rapids, MI: Eerdmans.

Lucas, E. (1996), *Science and the New Age Challenge*. Leicester: Apollos.

McDonald, H. D. (1981), *The Christian View of Man*. London: Marshall, Morgan & Scott.

McHarg, I. L. (1969), *Design with Nature*. New York: Doubleday.

MacKay, D. M. (1960), *Science and Christian Faith Today*. London: Falcon.

———————— (1974), *The Clockwork Image*. London: Inter-Varsity Press.

———————— (1978), *Science, Chance and Providence*. Oxford: Oxford University Press.

———————— (1979), *Human Science and Human Dignity*. London: Hodder & Stoughton.

———————— (1984), 'The Beginnings of Personal Life'. *In the Service of Medicine* 30.2:9–13.

McKay, K. L. (1982), 'Creation'. In *New Bible Dictionary*, 2nd edn: 245–248. Douglas, J. D. *et al.* (eds.). Leicester: Inter-Varsity Press.

McKibben, B. (1994), *The Comforting Whirlwind: God, Job, and the Scale of Creation*. Grand Rapids, MI: Eerdmans.

Mahoney, J. (1984), *Bioethics and Belief*. London: Sheed & Ward.

Man in His Living Environment (1969). London: Church House Press.

Mayr, E. (1991), *One Long Argument: Charles Darwin and the Genesis of Modern Evolutionary Thought*. London: Allen Lane.

Meadows, D. H., Meadows, D. L. & Randers, J. (1972), *The Limits to Growth*. New York: Universe Books.

Meadows, D. H., Meadows, D. L., Randers, J. & Behrens, W. W. (1992), *Beyond the Limits*. London: Earthscan.

Medawar, P. (1984), *The Limits of Science*. New York: Harper & Row.

————— (1990a), 'Is the Scientific Paper a Fraud? In *The Threat and the Glory*: 228–233. Oxford: Oxford University Press.

————— (1990b), 'Scientific Fraud'. In *The Threat and the Glory*: 64–70. Oxford: Oxford University Press.

Medina, J. (1991), *The Outer Limits of Life*. Nashville, TN: Oliver-Nelson.

Midgley, M. (1992), *Science as Salvation: A Modern Myth and its Meaning*. London: Routledge.

Monod, J. (1970), *Le Hasard et la nécessité*. Paris: Éditions du Seuil (Eng. trans. 1972, *Chance and Necessity*. London: Collins).

Montefiore, H. (ed.) (1975), *Man and Nature*. London: Collins.

————— (1985), *The Probability of God*. London: SCM.

Moore, N. W. (1987), *The Bird of Time: The Science and Politics of Nature Conservation*. Cambridge: Cambridge University Press.

Morgan, D. & Lee, R. G. (1991), *Blackstone's Guide to the Human Fertilization and Embryology Act, 1990*. London: Blackstone.

Morris, H. M. (1980), *King of Creation*. San Diego: Christian Literature Press.

Mott, N. (ed.) (1991), *Can Scientists Believe? Some Examples of the Attitude of Scientists to Religion*. London: James & James.

Moule, C. F. D. (1964), *Man and Nature in the New Testament*. London: Athlone.

————— (1965–6), 'St Paul and Dualism: The Pauline Conception of Resurrection'. *New Testament Studies* 13:106–123.

Murray, J. (1957), *Principles of Conduct*. London: Tyndale.

Myers, D. G. & Jeeves, M. A. (1987), *Psychology through the Eyes of Faith*. Leicester: Apollos.

Naess, A. (1989), *Ecology, Community and Lifestyle*. Cambridge: Cambridge University Press.

Nelson, J. R. (1994), *On the New Frontiers of Genetics and Religion*. Grand Rapids, MI: Eerdmans.

Nicholson, E. M. (1970), *The Environmental Revolution*. London: Hodder & Stoughton.

Norton, B. G. (1987), *Why Preserve Natural Variety?* Princeton, NJ: Princeton University Press.

Numbers, R. L. (1992), *The Creationists: The Evolution of Scientific Creationism*. New York: Alfred Knopf.

O'Donovan, O. M. T. (1984), *Begotten or Made?* Oxford: Oxford University Press.

Oelschlaeger, M. (1994), *Caring for Creation: An Ecumenical Approach to the Environmental Crisis*. New Haven: Yale University Press.

Osborn, L. (1993), *Guardians of Creation*. Leicester: Apollos.

Our Common Future (1987), The Report of the World Commission on Environment and Development (the Brundtland Report). Oxford and New York: Oxford University Press.

Our Responsibility for the Living Environment (1986). London: Church Information Office.

Pantin, C. F. A. (1968), *Relations Between the Sciences*. Cambridge: Cambridge University Press.

Peacocke, A. R. (1986), *God and the New Biology*. London: Dent.

Pearce, E. V. K. (1969), *Who Was Adam?* Exeter: Paternoster.

Penrose, R. (1989), *The Emperor's New Mind: Concerning Computers, Minds and the Laws of Physics*. Oxford: Oxford University Press.

——————(1994), *Shadows of the Mind: A Search for the Missing Science of Consciousness*. Oxford: Oxford University Press.

Personal Origins (1985), The Report of a Working Party on Human Fertilization and Embryology of the Board for Social Responsibility. London: Church Information Office.

Polanyi, M. (1969), *Knowing and Being*. London: Routledge & Kegan Paul.

Polkinghorne, J. C. (1983), *The Way the World Is*. London: SPCK.

——————(1989), *Science and Providence*. London: SPCK.

——————(1994), *Science and Christian Belief*. London: SPCK. (Published in US as *The Faith of a Physicist*. Princeton: Princeton University Press).

Poole, M. (1992), *Miracles: Science, the Bible and Experience*. London: Scripture Union.

Popper, K. (1978), 'Natural Selection and the Emergence of Mind'. *Dialectica* 32:339–355.

Porritt, J. & Winner, D. (1988), *The Coming of the Greens*. London: Collins.

Rambler, M. B., Margulis, L. & Tester, R. (eds.) (1989), *Global Ecology: Towards a Science of the Biosphere*. San Diego, CA: Academic.

Ramsey, P. (1975), *The Ethics of Fetal Research*. New Haven: Yale University Press.

Rogerson, J. W. (1985), 'Using the Bible in the Debate about Abortion'. In *Abortion and the Sanctity of Life:* 77–92. Channer, J. H. (ed.). Exeter: Paternoster.

Ross, H. (1994), *Creation and Time: A Biblical and Scientific Perspective on the Creation-Date Controversy.* Colorado Springs, CO: NavPress.

Russell, C. A. (1985), *Cross-Currents: Interactions between Science and Faith.* Leicester: Inter-Varsity Press.

————— (1989), 'The Conflict Metaphor and its Social Origins'. *Science and Christian Belief* 1:3–26.

————— (1994), *The Earth, Humanity and God.* London: UCL Press.

Sagoff, M. (1988), *The Economy of the Earth.* Cambridge: Cambridge University Press.

Schaeffer, F. (1970), *Pollution and the Death of Man.* London: Hodder & Stoughton.

————— (1973), *Genesis in Space and Time.* London: Hodder & Stoughton.

Schumacher, E. F. (1973), *Small is Beautiful.* London: Blond & Briggs.

Shute, N. (1957), *In the Wet.* London: Heinemann.

Singer, P. (1976), *Animal Liberation.* London: Jonathan Cape.

————— (1981), *The Expanding Circle: Ethics and Sociobiology.* Oxford: Clarendon.

Singer, P. & Wells, D. (1983), '*In Vitro* Fertilization: The Major Issues'. *Journal of Medical Ethics* 9:192–195.

Smuts, J. C. (1926), *Holism and Evolution.* London: Macmillan.

Spanner, D. C. (1965), *Creation and Evolution.* London: Falcon.

Stott, J. R. W. (1992), *The Contemporary Christian.* Leicester: Inter-Varsity Press.

————— (1994), *The Message of Romans.* Leicester: Inter-Varsity Press.

Sustainable Development: The UK Strategy (1994). London: Her Majesty's Stationery Office, Cm. 2426.

Teilhard de Chardin, P. (1959), *The Phenomenon of Man.* London: Collins.

This Common Inheritance: Britain's Environmental Strategy (1990). London: Her Majesty's Stationery Office. Cm. 1200.

Thorpe, W. H. (1961), *Biology, Psychology and Belief.* Cambridge: Cambridge University Press.

Trevelyan, G. M. (1938), *England under the Stuarts.* London: Methuen.

Trigg, R. (1993), *Rationality and Science: Can Science Explain Everything?* Oxford: Blackwell.

Triton, A. N. (1970), *Whose World?* London: Inter-Varsity Press.

Van Till, H. J., Snow, R. E., Stek, J. H. & Young, D. A. (1990), *Portraits of Creation: Biblical and Scientific Perspectives on the World's Formation*. Grand Rapids, MI: Eerdmans.

White, A. D. (1986), *A History of the Warfare of Science and Theology*. New York: Appleton.

White, L. (1967), 'The Historical Roots of our Ecologic Crisis'. *Science*, New York, 155:1204–1207.

Whitehouse, C. (1983), '*In Vitro Veritas?*' *Third Way* 6.9:24–27.

Wilkinson, D. (1993), *God, the Big Bang and Stephen Hawking*. Tunbridge Wells: Monarch.

Wilkinson, L. (ed.) (1991), *Earthkeeping in the 90s: Stewardship of Creation*. Grand Rapids, MI: Eerdmans.

Williams, B. (1985), 'Which Slopes are Slippery?' In *Moral Dilemmas in Modern Medicine*: 126–137. Lockwood, M. (ed.). Oxford: Oxford University Press.

Wilson, E. O. (1975), *Sociobiology: The New Synthesis*. Cambridge, MA: Belknap.

——————(1978), *On Human Nature*. Cambridge, MA: Harvard University Press.

Wiseman, P. J. (1948), *Creation Revealed in Six Days*. London: Marshall, Morgan & Scott.

Wolff, H. W. (1974), *Anthropology of the Old Testament*. London: SCM.

World Conservation Strategy (1980). Gland, Switzerland: International Union for the Conservation of Nature, United Nations Environmental Programme, World Wildlife Fund.

Wright, C. J. H. (1990), *God's People in God's Land: Family, Land and Property in the Old Testament*. Grand Rapids, MI: Eerdmans.

Wright, R. T. (1989), *Biology through the Eyes of Faith*. Leicester: Apollos.

Young. D. A. (1982), *Christianity and the Age of the Earth*. Grand Rapids, MI: Zondervan.

INDEX

Adam, 14, 32, 49–54, 74, 76, 103, 117, 120
altruism, 48, 62–63, 86
anthropic principle, 99
Archimedes, 26
argument from design, 13, 26, 36
Aristotle, 12, 21, 68, 72, 81
artificial insemination, viii, 66, 75–76, 78
Ashby, Eric, 86, 89–92
Assisi Declarations, 97, 101
Augustine, 16, 42–43, 51, 68, 77

Bacon, Francis, 12
behaviour genetics, 61
Bernal, J. D., 8
Big Bang, 111
books of God, 19, 77, 113, 116, 124
Boyle, Robert, 11
Brave New World, 59
Bridgewater Treatises, 14
Brown, Louise, 66–67
Brundtland Report, 90
Brunner, Emil, 49

Buffon, Comte de, 15, 17, 31

Cain (and his wife), 50
Calvin, John, 18, 31, 36, 39
cancer, 59, 72
catastrophe/catastrophism, 17, 33, 43, 91
Chalmers, Thomas, 43
Chambers, Robert, 33–34
chimpanzees, 29–30
chromosomes, 30, 59, 78–79
Chrysostom, 16
clean-air laws, 90–91
Code of Environmental Practice, 101
complementarity, 19–23, 31, 40, 45–46, 55, 116, 119–120
conflict between science and faith, 6, 38, 113
consciousness, viii, 120
continental drift, 34
Copernicus, Nicholas, 3, 18
creation ex nihilo, 6, 39, 41, 47, 102
creation ordinances, 122

creation spirituality, 98
criminality, 61
Cuvier, G., 17

Darwin, Charles, 4, 6, 14, 32–37, 62, 96
days of creation, 42–43, 112
death, 51, 104
dedivinization, 40, 96
deep ecology, 99–100
deism, 55
Delors, Jacques, 96
determinism, viii, 23, 59, 62, 98, 114, 119
dinosaurs, 37, 54
Disraeli, Benjamin, 48
DNA, 30, 59–60
domestication, 35, 49
dominion (over nature), 80, 94–96
donor insemination, 66, 75–76, 78
Down's syndrome, 61–62
duality, 76, 102

Earth, age of the, 14–15, 32, 37
Earth Charter, 101
Eden, Garden of, 14, 40–41, 50, 117
Einstein, Albert, 1, 90
emergent properties, 24
Enlightenment, the, 85, 95, 100
Enuma Elish, 41
epigenetics, 59–62
Essays and Reviews, 38
eugenics, 65
evangelism, 5, 8
Eve, 50–53, 103, 117, 120; see also Adam
Evelyn, John, 87

extinction, 16, 32, 43

fall, the, 51–54, 74, 98, 103–104, 118, 120
Faraday, Michael, 16
flood, the, 14, 16, 120
fossil, 14, 16–17, 31, 33–35, 43, 49, 120
Fox, Matthew, 98, 117
Francis of Assisi, 94
fraud, 26
free will, 23, 114, 120

Gaia, 99
Galileo Galilei, 7, 18–19, 73, 96, 113
Galton, Francis, 64
geographical distribution, 34–35
Gnosticism, 103
God of the gaps, 22, 106
God, too small, 55, 106, 244
Gödel's theorem, 120
Gosse, Philip, 14
Grand Unified Theory, 33
Gray, Asa, 36

Haldane, J. B. S., 8, 62, 119
healing, 45, 80, 115, 112
Heisenberg's uncertainty principle, 22
Heyerdahl, Thor, 55
Hobhouse, L. T., 48
Hodge, A. A., 36
holism, 24
homosexuality, 63
Hooker, Joseph, 35
Human Fertilization and Embryology Authority (HFEA), 7, 67, 78–80

Human Genome Project, 60
Hume, David, 25, 57
Huxley, Aldous, 59
Huxley, Julian, 103
Huxley, Thomas Henry, 4, 8, 37

image (of God), 11, 31, 48–49,
    52–53, 70, 76–77, 79, 83, 95,
    118, 122
immanence, 42, 55, 96, 102, 118,
    121
in vitro fertilization (IVF), vii, 66,
    76, 78
inerrancy, 116

Jenkins, David, 11
Jordan (river), 45

Kammerer, P., 35
Kepler, Johannes, 11, 40
Kidner, Derek, 40, 52–53
kin selection, 63
Kon Tiki, 55

Lamarck, J. D., 17, 31–32
land use, 87, 95
Laplace, Marquis de, 11–12
laws of science, 1, 12, 21, 33, 63
Leopold, Aldo, 95, 100
leprosy, 45
Lewis, C. S., 57, 99, 111, 119
Lewontin, R. C., 37
Lightfoot, John, 32
limits of science, 22
Limits to Growth, The, 89
Locke, John, 112
Luther, Martin, 33–34, 96
Lyell, Charles, 32–34, 96
Lysenko, T. D., 35

McHarg, Ian, 93–94
MacKay, Donald, 2, 20–21, 120
marriage, 66, 68, 74
Medawar, P., 22, 26–27
Mendel, Gregor, 35, 52
Midgley, Mary, 23
Milton, John, 112
miracles, viii, 1–3, 45, 55–56,
    110, 114
Monod, Jacques, 25, 29, 118
Mott, Neville, 8
Muir, John, 95, 100, 103

naked ape, 29
Napoleon, 11
Nature, 1–3, 19
neo-Darwinism, 6, 36
neolithic, 49–50, 52
New Age, 97–98, 100, 102
Newton, Isaac, 11, 15, 26
Noah, 14, 16
nothing-buttery, 20–22, 24, 29,
    54, 106, 119

omphalos, 14
Origen, 42
Origin of Species, The, 4, 33–35
Our Common Future, 90
over-population, 30, 88, 122
Owen, Richard, 37
ozone layer, 86

Paley, William, 13, 14, 102, 122
panentheism, 98, 102, 121, 124
pantheism, 39, 97–98, 121
Pantin, Carl, 24
paradigm, 36
Pascal, Blaise, 11
personhood, 70–71

Piltdown hoax, 31
plagues of Egypt, 45
Plato, 3, 17, 72, 119
playing God, 80
plenitude, 16
Polanyi, Michael, 20
Polkinghorne, John, viii, 25, 56
pollution, 86, 96, 100
pope, the, 19, 66, 68–69, 94
Popper, Karl, 22, 26, 101
Porter, George, 29, 55, 116
positivism, 22, 25
postmodernism, 106, 119
prayer, 45, 99, 123
process theology, 99, 102, 115, 123
providence, 36, 44–45, 68, 115
Ptolemy, 14, 18, 112, 119
Puritanism, 11–12

Ray, John, 12–13
Red Sea, crossing of, 45
reductionism, 23–25
resurrection, 1, 98, 116
Rio (Earth) Summit, 86, 93, 101, 106
Royal Society of London, 1, 11, 55
Russell, Bertrand, 118

Sacred Theory of the Earth, The, 14
Schaeffer, Francis, 42, 46
Scofield Bible, 43
scientific method, 19–20, 26, 36, 111, 119
sex choice, 65–66, 78
Shackleton, Ernest, 56
Silent Spring, 88
Singer, P., 63, 67

Small is Beautiful, 98
Smith, William, 17
Smuts, Jan Christian, 24
Smyth, Frank, 56
sociobiology, 63
soul, 17, 13, 69–70, 72, 76
Spencer, Herbert, 5, 34, 65
stewardship, 53, 85, 94–95, 101–103, 106, 117, 118, 124
Stoics, 7, 81, 88
Stott, John R. W., vii, 51
sustainable development, 90, 101

Taylor, Hudson, 114–115
Teilhard de Chardin, P., 25, 103, 121
Temple, Frederick, 45
Tertullian, 16, 102
test-tube baby, 66; see also in vitro fertilization
theodicy, 39
Theory of Everything, 23
thermodynamics, 54
This Common Inheritance, 85
Thomas Aquinas, 50, 69
Thorpe, W. H., 48
Times, The, 1, 29, 89
Torrey Canyon, 88
transcendence, 55, 96, 102, 118, 121
Transcendental Meditation, 98, 100
Trevelyan, G. M., 12
twins, 61, 72

uniformitarianism, 33
Ussher, Archbishop, 32, 49

Vesalius, 3

Vestiges of . . . Creation, The, 33–34
vestigial organs, 34–35
vicegerency, 53, 104
Vienna Circle, 25
virgin birth, 1
vitalism, 24–25
volcanoes, 15

Wallace, A. R., 34
Warfield, B. B., 36, 50
Warnock Committee, 67

watchmaker, divine, 13–14, 46, 102, 119, 122
Weissmann, A. F. L., 35
Westminster Confession, 5, 39
Whewell, W., 26
White, Lynn, 94, 104
Wilberforce, Samuel, 37, 48
wilderness, viii, 103
Wilson, E. O., 63
World Conservation Strategy, 90–93, 101

KING ALFRED'S COLLEGE
LIBRARY

Christians in Science

Christians in Science (CiS) is an organization that links together scientists who are committed Christians as well as those who are in some way professionally involved in the relationship between science and Christian belief (e.g. clergy who used to be scientists, those involved in science education, those simply interested in the science/faith interface, *etc.*).

Its aims are to:

— develop and promote clearly thought out Christian views on the nature, scope and limitations of science, and on the changing interactions between science and faith
— encourage Christians who are involved with science to maintain an active faith and to apply it in their professional lives
— to bring Christian thought on scientific issues into the public arena
— to communicate the gospel within the scientific community

CiS is affiliated to the Universities and Colleges' Christian Fellowship (UCCF), 38 De Montfort Street, Leicester LE1 7GP, UK.

It publishes the journal *Science and Christian Belief*, organizes conferences, local groups and an email discussion list.
Full details are on internet http://www.tcp.co.uk/~carling/cis.html

For further details, contact
   Mr Bennet McInnes
   Secretary, Christians in Science
   Atholl Centre
   Pitlochry
   Perthshire
   PH1 5BX, UK

Evangelical Environmental Network

The Evangelical Environmental Network (EEN) is a group of individuals – including environmentalists, scientists, and theologians – who are concerned about caring for God's creation. It exists to encourage those involved to care about God's world in practical ways, using the Bible as a guide to develop 'stewardship' principles, and to act on these principles rather than just talk or think about them.

EEN publishes a quarterly newsletter 'Creation Care' and has developed an internet site (http://www.tcp.co.uk/~carling/eenhome.html) and an email discussion list.

For further details, contact:
  Dr R C J Carling
  UK Evangelical Environmental Network
  Christian Impact
  St Peter's Church
  Vere Street
  London W1M 9HP
  United Kingdom
  Tel: +44–(0)171–629–3615
  Fax: +44–(0)171–629–1284
  email: carling@tcp.co.uk

American Scientific Affiliation

The American Scientific Affiliation (ASA) is a fellowship of men and women of science and disciplines that can relate to science who share a common fidelity to the Word of God and a commitment to integrity in the practice of science. ASA was founded in 1941 and has grown significantly since that time. The stated purpose of the ASA is "to investigate any area relating Christian faith and science" and "to make known the results of such investigations for comment and criticism by the Christian community and by the scientific community."

ASA publishes the journal *Perspectives on Science and Christian Faith* and runs conferences and local groups.

It has an internet page at http://ursa.calvin.edu/chemistry/ASA/and has an email discussion list.

For further details contact:
  Don Munro
  American Scientific Affiliation
  ASA
  P.O. Box 668
  Ipswich
  MA 01938–0668
  USA

Science and the New Age Challenge

ERNEST LUCAS

The New Age movement is an important element in contemporary challenges to the claim that modern science is the defining model of truth. Many in the movement believe that there are affinities between Eastern mysticism and new theories in the sciences, particularly the new physics. They claim that science, properly understood, supports New Age perspectives.

Ernest Lucas, a scientist and biblical scholar, looks at several key thinkers who have influenced New Age concepts and attitudes, including de Chardin, Capra, Sheldrake and Lovelock. His approach is thematic, describing and evaluating New Age approaches to truth and human knowledge, physics, biology, evolution and ecology. Particularly, and sympathetically, he considers its sophisticated, but flawed, search for a holistic view of scientific truth, human knowledge and spirituality, but he finds it in Christian rather than New Age faith.

190 pages   *Large Paperback*

Apollos